John Henry Newman's Rhetoric

American University Studies

Series XIV
Education

Vol. 21

PETER LANG
New York • Bern • Frankfurt am Main • Paris

John Britt

John Henry Newman's Rhetoric

Becoming a Discriminating Reader

PETER LANG
New York • Bern • Frankfurt am Main • Paris

Library of Congress Cataloging-in-Publication Data

Britt, John
    John Henry Newman's rhetoric : becoming a
discriminating reader / John Britt.
        p. cm. — (American university studies. Series XIV,
Education ; vol. 21)
            Bibliography: p.
            1. Newman, John Henry, 1801-1890 — Style. 2. English
language — Rhetoric. I. Title. II. Series.
PR5109.B7   1989   828'.809 — dc19   88-37916
ISBN 0-8204-1065-9   CIP
ISSN 0740-4565

CIP-Titelaufnahme der Deutschen Bibliothek

Britt, John:
John Henry Newman's rhetoric : becoming a
discriminating reader / John Britt. — New York;
Bern; Frankfurt am Main; Paris: Lang, 1989.
  (American University Studies: Ser. 14,
  Education; Vol. 21)
  ISBN 0-8204-1065-9

NE: American University Studies / 14

Reprinted by permission of *Daedalus*, Journal of the American
Academy of Arts and Sciences, "Science and Culture," Winter
1965, Vol. 94, No. 1, Cambridge, Massachusetts.

From ENGLISH PROSE STYLE by Herbert Reed.
Copyright © 1952 by Herbert Reed and renewed © by
Benedict Reed. Reprinted by permission of Pantheon
Books, a Division of Random House, Inc.

Printed by Weihert-Druck GmbH, Darmstadt, West Germany

DEDICATION

This work is dedicated to a person who is eloquent in all
of the ways Newman's teacher was eloquent as well as in all of
the ways Newman himself was eloquent: Jane Britt, my wife. And
to our children who, like her, endured the years of absence which
the pursuit of this **organon** demanded. "Which is better, God only
knows." Socrates put it as he defended himself before the Athenian
court, and this is the question I can ask about this pursuit
which cost so much.

Is enim est **eloquens**

That person, then, is eloquent

qui et

who is able to speak

humilia subtiliter, et

in earthly matters,   subtly

magna graviter, et

in important matters, seriously

mediocria temperate

in ordinary matters, temperately.

potest dicere.

Cicero, **Orator.**

ACKNOWLEDGEMENTS

The University of Dayton's School of Education's Dean, Ellis Joseph, through a grant, provided the services of Mrs. Barbara Day to type the photoready manuscript. Earlier Mrs. Carole Werbrich typed the material provided by Mrs. Bev Stoller who typed from an audiotape. During this time, I was blessed with an amanuensis, Mr. Charles Hewitt. Also I had Ms. Karen Vigre perfect the materials from the various typings in order that Mrs. Day would have a better manuscript from which to type. Without the Dean's faultless backing the present work would not exist.

The editors and the members of **Vitae Scholasticae** and the members of the Friends of Newman and **AESA**, the Foundations of Education society provided valuable criticism of the work during the earlier stages. Professor P. J. Corbett of Ohio State University, originally criticized the work prepared for **Vitae Scholasticae** and convinced me to begin on the **organon** approach which became the heart of the work. Mrs. Peggy Butts, from NCR, kept the work going by assisting in the original ordering of the material at a time when it seemed best to give up the project. Three readers - John Coratti, Jack Shaw, and Charles Hewitt - encouraged me to continue due to their acceptance of what I had begun. Mr. Michael Flamini, after I had worked with several editors in the university presses and in the religious presses, kept my enthusiasm going as did Ms. Hillary Wasserman and others at Peter Lang Publishing.

The librarians at the Marian Library and the Roesch Library, and especially those in the interlibrary loan section as well as the reference section gave unstintingly during the whole process. Faculty in the International Marian Research Institute, both here and in Rome, gave valuable assistance in working towards a better understanding of John Henry Newman.

My students worked through the various drafts as assignments and as the basis for lectures. Their understanding of Newman from the developing **organon** assured me that the approach was worth the effort. Any errors and lapses are due to my lacks and not to any of the devoted people who assisted me most cordially. My wife and children gave unstintingly of their time, concern, and love throughout the entire effort.

TABLE OF CONTENTS

INTRODUCTION

Problem

In a speech to the Royal Academy on May 3, 1890, some three months before Newman's death, John Morley praised literature and the English, then Cardinal Newman: "No prose more winning has ever been written than that of Cardinal Newman."[1] At about the same time, Augustine Birrell used John Morley's apology in the preface to his second book on Edmund Burke to prepare the audience for the limitations of his treatment of Burke before the Edinburgh Philosophical Society. Morley had noted that it is most difficult to say the same thing twice and well; therefore he quoted himself - in Greek. Birrell recognized the fact that the number of presentations extolling Burke was such that he would find it hard to say anything new well. Yet he found a way, which was to develop an analogy between Burke and Newman. "I have often been struck with a resemblance . . . between the attitude of Burke's mind toward government and that of Cardinal Newman toward religion. Both these great men belong, by virtue of their imaginations, to the poetic order, and they both are to be found dwelling with amazing eloquence, detail, and wealth of illustration on the varied elements of society. Both seem as they write to have one hand on the pulse of the world, and to be forever alive to the throb of its action; and Burke, as he regarded humanity swarming like bees into and out of their hives of industry, is ever asking himself, How are these men to be saved from anarchy? While Newman puts to himself the question, How are these men to be saved from atheism?"[2]

These passages provide an introduction and a link: these introduce us to principles, states of mind, and methods of thought as they provide a link between what will be written on these in John Henry Newman and other

authors. John Morley had studied the rhetoric on Edmund Burke most thoroughly, yet he could claim before the Royal Academy, a body of intellectuals
representing the highest in every area of pursuit, that Newman was equal
to the best persuasive writer of all time. His reason for this encomium
was to contrast the outstanding literature produced by those who devoted
all of their energies to the latter. Morley himself had sacrificed to enter
public life. The principle was clear: writing is a demanding taskmaster
and only total devotion enables one to be the best. His method of thought
was clear: parallel cases enable the listener to follow the argument and
the principle becomes clear at the point where the parallels cross. States
of mind were clear: Morley had experienced the two ways of life, many in
his audience had not and those had experienced Newman's dedication in their
own lives and all knew Newman's state of mind while Richard Hutton was on
the verge of publishing **John Henry Newman** in which this singleness of purpose
was highlighted as obvious to all, friend and foe.

The quotation from Birrell is sufficiently long to make the method
of thought, the states of mind, and the principles self-evident, but as
a check upon the reader's practice, it will help to note these. Once again
we have the use of parallel cases, of an analogy between the two great men;
we find the principles at the basis of comparison; and we have Burke's state
of mind in the fear of anarchy and Newman's state of mind in the fear of
atheism. Both saw themselves as warriors against the threat each realized
in the activities of their time.

In his **Apologia Pro Vita Sua**, Newman had won the English to his side
by revealing his unchanging battle with Liberalism: first, during the Oxford
Movement, by awakening Oxford while he was an Anglican and through Oxford

all of England and the United States; secondly, during his years as a Catholic in writing upon writing.

In the **Oxford University Sermons**, Newman had waged the war by inquiring into the ways people used the words "faith" and "reason." In the **Essay on Development of Christian Doctrine**, Newman worked out his own stand on the validity and the authority of the Church in England. In his first novel, **Loss and Gain**, he displayed the workings of Oxford from the perspectives of the students, the tutors, the administrators and the teachers during the time he was there. In **Callista**, he contrasted the period of the Fathers with his own by developing the issue of atheism in the African Church and in Rome. In the **Idea of a University**, Newman fought over the spirit of Edinburgh and Oxford under Copleston as well as over the place of religion in a university. In the **Grammar**, he took up the issue of atheism as he had raised it in the **Apologia** and prepared the way for both the educated and the uneducated in the conflict with the liberal challengers.

In order to enable the reader to become accomplished in determining the states of mind, the methods of thought, and the principles of Newman, we will select a sufficient number of specimens from these works and examine them in detail. Earlier Walter Houghton had done something of this type of analysis of the **Apologia**. Charles Harrold, then the leading Newman scholar in the United States, praised the **many ways** in which Newman's mind had worked. It is to follow up on Houghton and the criticism of him by Harrold that this work had been pursued. The present work aims to further the development of Houghton's masterpiece in light of Harrold's acute criticism.

Another author upon whom the present work depends is Francis Donnelly, who in **Imitation and Analysis** reminds the reader: "In composition, as in every other art, success begins with imitation. . . . It aims . . . to make another's writing yield up under close scrutiny and analysis certain laws, principles, methods, and devices of expression of which no writer has a monopoly, but which lie at the very root of all effective speech. . . . The student of composition as such turns to classic literature precisely because it realizes with obvious success those very laws and methods of expression which he himself must attend to in the presentation of his own thought under penalty of failure."[3]

Granted Newman does not have a monopoly on the "laws, principles, methods, and devices of expression," nonetheless an author deserving of the praise John Morley gave him before the Royal Academy has much to share through a close scrutiny.

This close scrutiny will not assure us of success. Two discoveries Newman prided himself upon were an awareness of antecedent reasoning and the illative sense. Just as the notional and real assents Newman caused to enter into the usual background knowledge of all writers of English need not be described, so the illative sense need not be. However an example of its importance will serve as the basis for a description and the basis of an issue those who accept the theory of imitation must face.

Houghton searched diligently and as perceptively as he was able for the states of mind in Newman's writings and, on occasion, had to confess he could not be sure, any more than Newman himself could have been. Regardless, Houghton and Harrold after him claimed that states of mind were more important for Newman than methods of thought. This paradoxical search raised a crucial issue: can we get beyond the illative sense, the idiosyncratic faculty of judgment, by means of our approach? Geoffrey Strickland compared Roland Barthes and Frank Leavis in **Structuralism or Criticism**.

Whereas Barthes moved from clear structural position further and further, Leavis answered those critics who asked for his criteria by an **ad hominem** argument based upon the illative sense: they knew the difference between the best and the mediocre whether they could put this difference in words. Strickland took a mean position: "Leavis's actual practice as a critic is, of course, the best clue to what he thought criticism was, and it will be generally argued that as a critic he was uncompromising in that he judged all writing by what he understood as the highest possible standard."[4] The point is we need clues.

Rather than to state what Newman did when he wrote, it is preferable to search for clues in his practice. This is, as we noted, what Houghton did and Harrold praised him for while faulting him for his brevity: there are **more ways** in which Newman's mind worked than the few Houghton demonstrated most articulately.

To determine how his mind worked we will use his own approach: "Here I end my specimens, among the many which might be given."[5] For Newman, a specimen was at once typical and something characteristic.

Since I wrote of Strickland's position, I have come upon substantiation for this in a famous critic of Newman, Leslie Stephen. "The critic has to be a prophet without inspiration. The one fact given him is that he is affected in a particular way by a given work of art; the fact to be inferred is, that the work of art indicates such and such qualities in its author, and will produce such an effect upon the world. No definite mode of procedure is possible. It is a question of tact and instinctive appreciation; it is not to be settled by logic, but by what Dr. Newman calls the 'illative sense;' the solution of the problem is to be felt out, not reasoned out, and the feeling is necessarily modified by the 'personal equation,' by that particular modification of the critic's own faculties, which cause him to see things in a light more or less peculiar to himself."[6]

Overview

Martin Amis wrote in "Broken Lance," his review of **Don Quixote** in the March 1986 **The Atlantic**, ". . . it should be stressed that when a great book enters a period of dormancy in any particular age, then the age is the loser; the age is judged, as well as the book."[7]

John Henry Cardinal Newman, 1801 - 1890, left us several great books. Our age is all but blind to them and the age out of which they came. But Karen Lawrence in **The Odyssey of Style in Ulysses** reminds us that James Joyce considered Newman the finest prose writer in English. Her literary evidence comes out of **The Portrait of the Artist as a Young Man**, Joyce's letters, and a section of **Ulysses** wherein Joyce presented an epitome of style and used one of Newman's sermons as his model. Joyce's age was alive to Newman. And in our age, Bernard Lonergan utilized Newman as a central source of themes and inspiration in his major work **Insight**, and in the development of his later thought. But today's educators, writers, and thinkers, and consequently the students of the university, as a whole have little or no awareness of Newman.

Major Purpose

The major purpose I have in examining Newman's writings is to make our age aware of these great books in a critical manner.

James Collins, a historian of philosophy and a critic of Newman, made two helpful suggestions for such study. It is best not to try to go through all of him, but to take themes; and it is best to take him up on his own terms. In that way, what he has to offer will bear upon our own time.

Incorporating these suggestions in my own work, I have contemplated Newman's writings as more than an art form. His purpose is to arouse his readers to examine their **beliefs** by a clear presentation of his experience.

Once I realized Newman's handling of themes, I grasped his tremendous tolerance of error, due to his conviction that error was in certain circumstances the way to truth. Truth meant everything to him. This ultimate principle manifests itself in all of Newman's works. Creatures will go off mistakenly, but to the point that they have good will they will be open to conversion and persuasion. Their roads will appear contrary to many, confusing to some, but they will converge.

Newman's handling of themes is an art. This art becomes lustrous due to his permeating principles, his ability to put himself in another's state of mind, and his skill in handling a complex variety of methods of thought. These are evident in that work Walter Pater claimed was "the perfect handling of a theory like Newman's **Idea of a University.**"[8] But they also appear in the **Apologia Pro Vita Sua,** his defense of his conversion from Anglicanism to Catholicism.

Through his researches into **The Arians of the Fourth Century,** Newman came to approach the theological dimensions of the Church, catholicity and apostolicity. Although Newman's essential assent in believing in God never wavered, his mode of belief and of accepting the truth of Catholic faith via the early Church revolutionized his Anglican point of view and led him to the Roman Catholic Church. Newman responded to Charles Kingsley's charge not only for the protection of his own clerical and scholarly reputation, but for the defense of the faith. Newman intended to speak to posterity, and paved a way for ecumenism.

Newman wrote **An Essay in Aid of a Grammar of Assent,** to reveal his discoveries and the philosophical underpinnings of faith and reason, as well as how the words "assent," "inference," and "certitude," are used in English and what they mean. Thus his book is a trial, an experiment, or an Essay to aid others in the way that Newman means and uses assent and still claims consistency and honesty of principles, as his **Apologia** had argued.

Newman wrote **The Idea of a University,** in which he detailed the theory of liberal education and investigated the values which could have averted "modernism." In this book, he pitted utilitarianism against liberal education, showed the place of theology in a university.

Secondary Purpose

My secondary purpose is to provide the teacher of prose style the epitome of a subtle writer which Sir Henry Craik praised ineluctably: His style is at once "simple and subtle" because of "the writer's beautiful and subtle mind." From the workings of his mind come the thoughts, "which it clothes in light and transparent vestures."[9] This style, as is clear from Herbert Read's **English Prose Style,** is that of an introvert.

Newman narrated rather than argued; expressed his thoughts rather than considered their impression; imagined rather than fancied; and sought unity rather than elegance. The fact that Newman's works yet explain, indicates how indirect argument can achieve what an extraverted directness often misses. In like manner, the values of Newman's opposite he nonetheless gained. Hence whether the reader favors the extraverted or the introverted approach to writing, Newman is a helpful example.

A reader would most probably know of Newman's **Apologia** and if not the review of Houghton and Harrold on **The Art of Newman's Apologia** should inform

those who do not. For the latter group Newman found a playful way to introduce the issue.

Newman published his "Reflections" on the Kingsley's apology in which
he put Kingsley against himself in the form of a dialogue.

> Mr. Kingsley relaxes: "Do you know, I like your
> **tone**. From your **tone** I rejoice, greatly rejoice, to
> be able to believe that you did not mean what you said."
>
> I rejoin: "**Mean** it! I maintain I never **said** it,
> whether as a Protestant or as a Catholic."
>
> Mr. Kingsley replies: "I waive that point."
>
> I object: "Is it possible? What? Waive the main
> question! I either said it or I didn't. You have made
> a monstrous charge against me; direct, distinct, public.
> You are bound to prove it as directly, as distinctly,
> as publicly;--or to own you can't."
>
> "Well," says Mr. Kingsley, "if you are quite sure
> you did not say it, I'll take your word for it; I really
> will."
>
> My **word**! I am dumb. Somehow I thought that it
> was my **word** that happened to be on trial. The **word**
> of a Professor of lying, that he does not lie!
>
> But Mr. Kingsley reassures me: "We are both
> gentlemen," he says. "I have done as much as one English
> gentleman can expect from another."
>
> I begin to see: he thought me a gentleman at the
> very time that he said I taught lying on system. After
> all, it is not I, but it is Mr. Kingsley who did not
> mean what he said. "Habemus confitentem reum."[10]

This led Kingsley to "What, Then, Does Dr. Newman Mean." That pamphlet
would be the final straw, giving Newman justification for publishing his
notes, letters, diaries and ideas in the form of the **Apologia Pro Vita Sua**.
Not only did he answer each specific charge Kingsley made in "What, Then,
Does Dr. Newman Mean," but he revealed his changing states of mind and the
principles guiding his life up through the time of his conversion to
Catholicism.

Charles Kingsley was right on one thing: "No man knows the use of words better than Dr. Newman; no man, therefore, has a better right to define what he does, or does not, mean by them."[11] We can learn the use of words from him merely by reading him, yet our experience is that only those who have learned the use of words exceedingly well read him. This misfortune must be corrected and in our day of methods or of how to do things, a remedy might be to teach those who have not dared to read him a simple way to do this. Another remedy might be to offer those who have the mission to teach those who have not dared to read Newman a simple way which has succeeded with such.

We will assume two things: that Newman is his best introduction and that any literate person is as capable of reading him as any other author; therefore we will use the following approach. Each stage in this book will be introduced by a specimen from one of Newman's major writings. After the passage, there will be a series of indications of how to get the most from the selection by means of three searches - a search for the states of mind, a search for the methods of thought, and a search for principles.

> This was my state of mind, as it had been for many years, when, in the beginning of 1864, I unexpectedly found myself publicly put upon my defense, and furnished with an opportunity of pleading my cause before the world, and, as it so happened, with a fair prospect of an impartial hearing. Taken by surprise, as I was, I had much reason to be anxious how I should be able to acquit myself in so serious a matter; however, I had long had a tacit understanding with myself, that, in the improbable event of a challenge being formally made to me, by a person of name, it would be my duty to meet it. That opportunity had now occurred; it never might occur again; not to avail myself of it at once would virtually give up my cause; accordingly, I took advantage of it, and, as it has turned out, the circumstance that no time was allowed me for any studied statements had compensated, in the equitable judgment of the public, for such imperfections in composition as my want of leisure involved.[12] (Read that passage out loud).

Thus did Newman introduce his classic **History of My Religious Opinions** in 1865, a year after he had rushed to meet the weekly journal publication deadlines between April 21st and June 12th and which he put out again in 1873 as **Apologia Pro Vita Sua: Being a History of His Religious Opinions**.

The ordinary reader can feel the drama of this defense and hear the rhythm of these sentences. On the other hand one might miss the significance of this claim of knowing his state of mind. Through some twenty years, Newman had felt the sting of calumny! Friend and foe had assumed to read his mind and convict him of dishonesty; nonetheless, as the **Apologia** convinced most readers, Newman was pursuing the truth at an enormous cost. Only if he could reveal his state of mind would he be able to win an acquittal before the public; he who had been convicted of libel against a publicly renowned liar, Achilli. No wonder a few years later he was anxious about acquitting himself.

The method of thought in this passage is rhetorical. Newman asked the readers to be impartial in examining his defense. He knew that the public was upset at the partiality shown against him in his recent trial. He knew that there were early and late prejudices against him. By willingly taking on the challenge of a renowned author and clergyman, he expected to use their feelings of guilt and their admiration for his courage in revealing his changing states of mind. Thus he bracketed the challenge and its acceptance with a confidence in the impartiality of his audience.

The principle in this passage is that he had a cause - to defend truth. He had come home from abroad in 1833 with an assurance that he had a mission in England. This mission was known to every Englishman as the Oxford Movement, a reformation of the Anglican Church and an encounter with Liberalism. His own change of state of mind had led him to leave the Anglican Church and to allow the advocates of Liberalism to gain the upper hand at Oxford. Now he could defend his cause: the truth of the Church and the falsity of Liberalism. In doing so, he would defend himself and his honesty as he defended the priesthood.

The first page of the **Apologia** describes Newman's state of mind at the beginning of 1864 when Charles Kingsley finally provided him with an opportunity to defend himself against the charge of a lack of "simplicity and uprightness" during the years he was an Anglican. This state of mind was that which a sensitive person would have as a result of the startling act he carried out in 1845 - his conversion from the Anglican religion to the Catholic. A chief ingredient in this state of mind was his necessary acceptance of the suspicion resting in the minds of the people of England from the fact that for a long period of time Newman had charged Roman Catholics with a failure by which he justified Anglicans and kept them from seeking union with her, and then he joined her.

He was conscious, in a state of mind, that his conversion had deeply hurt those with whom he had the closest ties; his family, his Oxford friends, and his Anglican associates and parishioners. Only a complete disclosure of his development would heal the breach. Only such would enable him to regain a state of mind in which he would feel able to meet with those former friends in a renewed bond of trust. And this disclosure of his development would have to be personal, whereas his **Essay on the Development of Christian Doctrine** had been academic and his novel, **Loss and Gain**, had been literary. Here he would have to be himself openly and simply if he were to persuade the groups prejudiced against him.

Probably the single most telling difference between a Protestant and a Catholic form of Anglicanism was the acceptance or rejection of the notes of the Church, especially on antiquity and sanctity. It was this difference in principle which brought a rupturing state of mind to Newman as he retreated to Littlemore. As he recalled: "Our Church teaches the Ancient faith. I did not conceal this: in Tract 90, it is put forward as the first principle of all. It is a duty which we owe both to the Catholic Church, and to our own, to take our reformed confessions in the most Catholic sense they will admit; we have no duties towards their framers."[13]

This principle began as an intellectual perfection. He knew that the long experience of his Church was divided between those who depended upon the interpretation dependent upon the intention of the writers and those who depended upon the belief of the Church as such, yet he pushed the principle which put the weight on the "belief of the Catholic Church as such." Those who feared he was moving from Anglicanism to Rome read his Tract 90 as a clear signal. With this principle in mind, it is easier to return to the most significant statement of his state of mind at the beginning of Chapter III: History of my religious opinions from 1839 to 1841, "And now I am about to trace . . ."[14]

Gordon Harper interpreted the issue in Newman and Froude as follows:

> It was six years before Newman finally gave to the problem of reasonable religious belief the solution which had been developing in his mind since the delivery of his **University Sermons.** The Trinity in the **Grammar of Assent** had its roots in the lecture hall of Oxford when Newman had first read Butler's **Analogy,** a book which perhaps more strongly than any other had influenced a generation of Oxford men. Hurrell Froude too had drawn much of his intellectual inspiration from it, and in this official capacity as tutors at Oriel both of them had so implanted in William the dictum of Butler's that probability is the guide of life, that it formed the permanent basis of his later thought. From this common point William Froude and Newman set out upon different courses and travelled always farther apart; and yet a careful examination of the progress of each one would probably reveal no error of logic, proving what Newman had always maintained, that from

a single source two logical minds might nevertheless diverge.

Newman's philosophical creed in regards to religious belief relegated reason (by which he meant, with Coleridge, the **Verstand**, the power of proceeding logically in intellectual matters) to a place secondary to faith, while in his conception amounted to a kind of super-reason not unlike Coleridge's conception of **Vernunft**. A fundamental point of his belief was that one attains religious truth differently from the way one arrives at truth in secular manners.

For attaining supernatural truth a particular disposition or quality of mind was indispensable.[15]

In 1839, Newman was convinced he should develop an essay "Prospects of the Anglican Church" which he noticed in the **Apologia**. This essay gave a defense of the Oxford Movement against charges by "ultra-Protestants" that it was a mere party. The defense explicates how a common movement can result without plan or conspiracy. Instead a principle has a momentum of its own, or as he put it, "You cannot make others think as you will, no, not even those who are nearest and dearest to you. And if you cannot do this, if principles will develop themselves, beyond the arbitrary points of which you are so fond, and by which they have hitherto been limited, like prisoners on parole, then it becomes a piece of practical wisdom to take what you can get."[16]

This principle of the Oxford Movement, "the spiritual awakening of spiritual wants"[17] began some one hundred years before its flowering. By returning to the Fathers of the Church, by returning to Antiquity, the Anglicans hoped to forestall a movement towards Roman Catholicism. Newman lists a number of members of the movement who came from a variety of religious persuasions with an enormous variety of prejudices, antecedent probabilities and so on, yet who shared a common state of mind, a state of mind in search of what was its due. Not that they wanted to go back, but they wanted what was rightly theirs that had been covered over by the Reformation.

This state of mind became sufficiently explicit that those of a liberal position could combat it. They could expose tendencies towards this state of mind in the Oxford University, in the preaching of its members, and in the tracts they published as well as in their political moves to change society.

And the liberals with no religion or with the general religion of England could recognize the differences of the principle of the Oxford Movement from the Protestant principle. The Bible was not enough for Puseyites; sacraments and authority were necessary. Private judgment, then, was inadequate. Rather than accepting single verses from Scripture, they read the Word as a whole and they depended upon the authority of the bishops rather than upon their own.

By reading Newman with this contrast of principle, state of mind, and methods of thought in mind, one can feel the controversy and accept its significance for him. The recent work of Innis, McLuhan, and Ong on the difficulty of separating ourselves from our surroundings came through in Newman's criticism of Scott and Coleridge and his extolling of Knox. (Note, this also helps us understand Vico's rejecting of Descartes).

"Such is the prophecy of a calm and sagacious mind, whose writings are themselves no slight evidence of the intellectual and moral movement under consideration. In this respect he outstrips Scott and Coleridge, that he realizes his own position."[18]

Scott and Coleridge are used in comparison since they prepared the English mind for the Oxford Movement, but they did this without, Newman indicated, knowing their own position. They set the stage for others to fulfill their spiritual wants by opening the hidden treasure without realizing

what they were doing. They fulfilled the principle and added to its momentum
while freeing the current not by recognizing the cause of the current nor
their own need for it.

Newman was aware of this difference in approach to a changed state
of mind by a close study of the three noted writers: an autobiographer,
a novelist, and a literary critic. Their styles and their genres were different while their participation in this long term movement was one.

States of Mind and Principle:
The Setting of the Diamond - **The Idea of a University**

If Newman handled the theory of a university perfectly as Walter Pater
stressed in his work on style, we would expect to find the **correct setting
for the diamond - The Idea of a University.** It is itself in section 1 of
Discourse V. The introductory chapter outlines four reasons for his acceptance of the challenge of starting a Catholic University in Dublin, then
it raises the objections to the project, and concludes that obedience to
the authority of the Irish bishops and the Pope should enable a unity of
effort as the Irish and the English saved the intellectual light for Europe
centuries before. Discourses II - IV care for the first of the two questions
posed at the opening, "Whether it is consistent with the idea of a university
teaching to exclude theology from a place among the sciences which it
embraces."[19]

After considering Theology as a branch of knowledge, its bearing on
other branches of knowledge, and the bearing of other branches of knowledge
on Theology, he considered he had said "enough in proof of the first point."
This led to Discourses V - VIII:

> A University may be considered with reference to
> its students or to its studies; and the principle, that
> all knowledge is a whole and the separate sciences parts
> of one, which I have hitherto been using in behalf of

> its studies, is equally important when we direct our
> attention to its students, and shall consider the
> education which, by virtue of this principle, a University
> will give them; and thus I shall be introduced, Gentlemen,
> to the second question . . . whether and in what sense
> its teaching, viewed relatively to the taught, carries
> the attribute of utility along with it.[20]

The unity of the work is evident in this introductory sentence of Discourse V. One **Principle** pervades the entire search. Just as a two-fold unity pervades the **Apologia Pro Vita Sua**, apologetic and autobiographical, so the wholeness of knowledge is the source of the unity of the **Idea**. Here, too, the state of mind is joined with the principles because the sciences are - "The acts and the work of the creator complement and fulfill one another." "This consideration, if well-founded, must be taken into account, not only as regards the attainment of truth, which is their common end, but as regards the influence which they exercise upon those whose education consists in the study of them." This latter is the state of mind which pervades the second set of four discourses. As the subjects form an ultimate unity, likewise they influence a unity among the students.

This point becomes clearer by a digression. Version is the medical term for the rotation of the fetus in the womb. Socrates, the midwife, made this analogous to the role of the teacher. Plato made this his definition of education: conversion in the readiest way possible. They found the way to this by conversation. From Plato's Academy to Newman, we have the university as a place of conversion from illusion to reality, from falsity to truth, from ignorance to knowledge by way of inquiry.

The remainder of section 1 leads towards two points: a definition of education as "Liberal" and the question which will guide the inquiry.

1. "Education is called 'Liberal.' A habit of mind is formed which lasts through life, of which the attributes are freedom, equitableness,

calmness, moderation, and wisdom . . . a philosophical habit." And, 2. "What is the **use** of it?"

Section 2 argued that "Knowledge is capable of being its own end . . . its own reward . . . true also of that special philosophy, which I have made to consist in a comprehensive

> **view** of truth in all its branches,
>> of the relations of science to science,
>> of their mutual bearings, and
>>> their respective values."

Thus Newman enlarged upon his definition of Liberal Education by his use of "view" which is virtually a synonym for state of mind. Once again the principle and the state of mind coalesce and the parallel brings out the fact that such knowledge is good rather than useful.

Section 3 expressed Cicero's argument for liberal education and against utilitarian education.

Section 4 gave Aristotle's argument. Newman introduced it by a powerful analogy uniting Cicero's reason for objecting to Cato and Aristotle's for objecting to Agathon.

"Things, which can bear to be cut off from everything else and
> yet persist in living,
>> must have life in themselves;
pursuits,
> which issue in nothing,
>> and still maintain their ground for ages,
> which are regarded as admirable,
>> though they have not as yet proved themselves
>>> to the useful,

must have their sufficient end in themselves,

    whatever it turns out to be."

After cataloguing instances of liberal knowledge and servile arts, he came to the principle Aristotle had given him:

"That alone is liberal knowledge,

    which stands on its own pretensions,

    which is independent of sequel,

      expects no complement,

      refuses to be **informed** (as it's called)

        by any end,

      or absorbed into any art,

   in order to duly present itself to our contemplation."

Section 5, the setting for the definition has included structure, principles, methods of thought, and state of mind welded together intricately. Thus we are not surprised to read: "There have indeed been differences of opinion from time to time, as to what pursuits and what arts came under that idea, but such differences are but an additional evidence of its reality. That idea must have a substance in it, changes,

      which had maintained its ground amid these conflicts

        and

      which has ever served as a standard to measure things

        withal,

      which has passed from mind to mind unchanged,

        when there was so much to colour,

            so much to influence every notion

        or thought whatever, which was not founded in

          our very nature."[21]

Section 6 divided Education by its methods into 1) philosophical, tending towards general ideas, and 2) mechanical, tending towards the particular. Why? Because when Newman considered Knowledge he meant

something intellectual,

something which grasps what it perceives through the senses;

something which takes a view of things;

which sees more than the senses convey;

which reasons upon what it sees, and

while it sees;

which invests it with an idea.[22]

For him, "This germ within knowledge of a philosophical process is the principle of real dignity in knowledge." The pursuit of such knowledge is what makes education a state of mind.

Sections 7 and 8 removed remaining objections by carrying out an examination of misunderstanding of what liberal education is and using the Philosophy of Utility itself as a means to safeguard the limits of liberal knowledge. He did this first by bringing out the Philosophy of Utility's mission: to "increase . . . physical enjoyment and social comfort."[23] Next he used an **ad hominem** argument against Bacon to clear the way for what could be expected of the utilitarian approach. The argument recounts Bacon's conviction of bribery.

Great as his insights, there was no necessary relationship between it and morality. There was no inconsistency, then, between Bacon developing a Utilitarian approach to life and his immorality because the two were completely incommensurate. Hence the way was cleared to conclude: "His is simply a method whereby bodily discomfort and temporal wants are to be most effectually removed from the greatest number. . . . Useful knowledge, then,

I grant, has done its work; and Liberal knowledge as certainly has not done its work."

Through this **false** and ironic parallel, Newman set the stage to present the limits of Liberal knowledge. His method of thought was to enter into the position of the objectors and use the very distinction his **ad hominem** argument had prepared those of a utilitarian mind to accept as if it were his position. If Bacon could develop an approach irrespective of morality and religion, so could Liberal education. "I consider knowledge to have its end in itself . . . it is so real a mistake to burden it with virtue or religion as with the mechanical arts." "Liberal education makes not the Christian, not the Catholic, but the gentleman."

Discourse VI cared for the definition of liberal education, of philosophy as an enlargement or enlightenment of the mind. Section 6, the highlight of this Discourse, is elaborately developed, as other material shows, but section 8 stresses the reason for his greatest labors on the behalf of education: "Education is a high word: it is the preparation for knowledge, and it is the imparting of that knowledge in proportion to that preparation."

Discourse VIII accepted the implications of his principle: the good is always useful, but the useful is not always good. This issue is treated later in a test case on principles, states of mind, and methods of thought.

Discourse VIII provided the issue more fully developed in his **Grammar** that religion is both philosophical and revealed. Liberal education can only go so far as the former which Newman's famous definition of the gentleman made clear.

Discourse IX is an epilogue. Once reason had gone as far, unaided, as it could, the responsibility of the Church became an issue. God, man, and nature constitute reality. Man, as Literature, and nature, as Science are directionless without God. The Church has to safeguard subjects and students from their tendencies towards making knowledge their own end.

Visual Approach to the **Idea**

With the summary and setting of the **Idea** covered it is well to show the elaborate approach Newman took to his subject by expressing his specimens in a visual manner. Below, we have an introduction to Newman's style, visual, on the one hand, oral/aural, on the other.

Structural Specimen

It is the education which gives man

a clear conscious view of his own opinions and judgements,

a truth in judging them,

an eloquence in expressing them, and

a force in urging them.

It teaches him

to see things as they are,

to go right to the point,

to disentangle a skein of thought

to detect which is sophisticated, and

to discard what is irrelevant. . . .

It shows him

how to accommodate himself to others,

how to throw himself into their state of mind,

how to bring before them his own,

how to influence them,

how to come to an understanding with them,

how to learn with them.[24]

Rhythm Specimen

He is at home in every society,

        he has common ground with every class;

he knows when to speak and

        when to be silent;

he is able to converse,

        he is able to listen;

he can ask a question patiently and

        gain a lesson seasonably

    when he has nothing to impart himself;

he is ever ready,

        yet never in the way;

he is a pleasant companion, and

        a comrade you can depend upon;

he knows when to be serious and

        when to trifle.

And he has a sure tact which enables him

        to trifle with gracefulness and

        to be serious with effect.

He has the repose of a mind which lives in itself,

        while it lives in the world,

And which has resources for its happiness at home

        when it cannot go abroad.

He has a gift which serves him in public,

        and supports him in retirement,

    without which good fortune is but vulgar,

and with which failure and disappointment have a charm.

> The art which tends to make a man all this,
>
> > is in the object which it perceives as useful
>
> > > as the art of wealth
> > >
> > > or the art of health,
>
> > though it is less susceptible of method,
>
> > > and less tangible,
> > >
> > > > less certain,
> > > >
> > > > less complete in its result.[25]

In light of the visual structure and in the sound of the aural rhythm, we can summarize the **Idea's** basis in Newman's rhetoric: **The Idea of a University** faced the issue of the continuity of Socrates' conviction: the unexamined life is not worth living. Plato, first, and Aristotle next, extended this to literature and to science. Newman accepted the issue at his time as the relation of God, man, and nature. He also accepted the challenges of his time: a Godless and utilitarian basis for education. In order to meet these challenges, he took an intuitive-introverted approach. In this, unity is the principal concern. This he found in God as Creator of man and nature. Next was his need for expressing his years of experience as a participant and an observer of the search for truth and meaning. Everything became autobiographical. All the characters in his drama were heroes and villains he had known or met in his study. Hence his discourses became narratives of the conflicts his imagination had dramatized. These characters and conflicts meant less to his audience than to those of Oxford but they symbolized similar characters and conflicts. Thus in completing a discourse, he could ask his hearers to continue the drama in their own minds.

As an intuitive-introvert, Newman recognized the need to communicate with extraverts, those who preferred argument, impressionism, fancy, and eloquence. Newman's eloquence came from his intense personal concern for liberal education. Despite his natural aversion to repetition, he discovered one set of descriptive arguments after another to make a point. For him this was necessary if his audience were to understand, but for other introverts it had the appearance of subtlety or paradox or even of magic. Those who were convinced upon the first occasion could well have been turned off by the repetition, yet Newman's methods of thought were cloaked in an artificial structure more evident to the **eye** than to the **ear**. His conversational style balanced the demands of the extravert and the introvert. Once again, for the extravert, he brought forth from his imaginative memory illustrations and examples which made his arguments seem objective. He impressed his audience with a feeling that this history of an idea was something passed on, a tradition inherited, a voice from those who had been there, not a mere subjective remembrance of an Oxford and an Anglican past.

Putting himself in the dual states of mind of his audience and his detractors, Newman embodied the very point he made. A gentleman could tolerate principles opposed to his, states of mind of mind at variance with his, and methods of thought beyond his grasp. He did not have to be the whole idea, he could share from those who differed from him and they should show themselves to be gentlemen. Frequently he called them by that name. They **were** where he wanted a university to bring others.

Specimens

Presentation of the materials in the form of **specimens** is necessary for introducing the reader to Newman, because he is dramatic and circumstantial. The reader must become involved in his witnessing, whether he or she agrees or disagrees; and this involvement increases by a consideration of his writings in light of principles, states of mind, and methods of thought.

In addition, this form lends itself most readily to give the materials for mastering Newman. Newman wrote in an organic style. Since he seldom wrote without a stimulus and since the stimulus involved a tension, a dramatic situation, he shared this situation with us. Thus, though the works of Newman are brilliantly clear in themselves, their hidden and fuller meanings require comparison of what else he had written on the same topic. Only a comparison of his many works will give the adequate meaning to any one of them.

By means of analyzing the principles, states of mind, and methods of thought of Newman the reader can grasp Newman's meaning, despite complaints that Newman is too subtle, cunning, and equivocal for accurate assessment.

This union of thought, meaning, and style is rooted in what Newman claimed was the **unum necessarium** in his lecture "University Preaching" - singleness of purpose. In one paragraph sometimes are collected a number of loose clauses, some no doubt being the interlineations of which he tells us, "all pointing in different directions, which, when the paragraph has been traversed, are seen to meet in a single point." By his singleness of purpose, Newman joined the comprehensive thought at which readers marvel with a clarity of expression which is sometimes awe-inspiring. Despite the prodigious labors he spent in re-writing and re-working his books and sermons, the finished writing appears almost facile. Newman claimed that style is the result of a union of thought and expression. The organic style best corresponds to his superb willingness to achieve this unity. No one knew better than he that none of his works, much less any one else's books, would ever be the last word on anything.

Thus I present the materials and the approaches necessary to understanding and mastering John Henry Newman. Not to say that other methods will not work as effectively in presenting Newman to new readers, students, and teachers, but that this method works best for me; this method of pursuing principles, states of mind, and methods of thought is geared toward the classroom as well as the individual; this method is encompassing in its scope, and yet flexible enough to permit detailed and focused examinations of individual parts. My handling of Newman is very like his own handling of knowledge, which he describes in Section 2 of Discourse III in his **Idea of a University**, ". . . as we deal with some huge structure of many parts and sides, the mind goes round about it, noting down, first one thing, then another, as it best may, and viewing it under different aspects, by way of making progress towards mastering the whole."

My methods for dealing with Newman, principles, states of mind, and methods of thought, consist of a **novum organon** for contemporary study of masters past and present. I discovered this process, this **novum organon**, through careful consideration of many authors and critics, notably Walter Pater, Walter Houghton, Herbert Read, and especially Newman himself.

I selected specimens from any one of the three only to find the others included. After working through this approach a number of times, the reader will catch on to the organon and be able to do it alone, for Newman or any other classical author.

Principles

By examining many crucial specimens, we come to grasp principles. For Newman they are the few but necessary starting points that give one's attempts at understanding the world a life-force, a sustaining movement. Newman wrote "Principles have a life and power independently of their authors, and make their way in spite of them; this at least is our philosophy."[26]

An example of a principle is in the introduction of Discourse V of the **Idea**. "A university may be considered with reference to either its students or its studies; and the principle, that all knowledge is a whole and the separate sciences are parts of one, which I have been hitherto using in behalf of its studies, is equally important when we direct our attention to its students."

Newman also told us his principle **vis a vis** belief, in the **Grammar**, Section 1 of "Belief in one God," ". . . in order to do this, of course I must start from some first principle; and that first principle, which I assume and shall not attempt to prove, is that which I should also use as a foundation in those other two inquiries [above], viz., that we have by nature a conscience."

"I assume . . . that Conscience has a legitimate place among our mental acts; . . . [and] in this special feeling . . . lie the materials for the real apprehension of a divine sovereign and judge."

And thirdly, Newman revealed his principle of faith in the **Apologia**. In the beginning of Part V, "And now that I am about to trace . . . the course of that great revolution of mind, . . . I feel overcome with the difficulty. . . . For who can know himself, and the multitude of subtle influences which act upon him?" Then, after analyzing the course of his separation from the Oxford Movement and the church of his childhood, he said in the fifth paragraph of Part VII of the **Grammar**:

> Starting . . . with the being of a God, (which, as I have said, is as certain to me as the certainty of my own existence, though when I try to put the grounds of that certainty into logical shape I find a difficulty in doing so in mood and figure to my satisfaction), I look out of myself into the world . . . which fills me with unspeakable distress. The world seems simply to give the lie to that great truth, . . . and . . . as a matter of necessity, [the effect] is as confusing as if it denied that I am in existence myself. . . . This

is . . . one of the great difficulties of this absolute primary truth. . . .

Newman was also aware of the difficulty in catching the principle in his "General Answer to Mr. Kingsley," saying

> But if we would ascertain with correctness the real course of a principle, we must look at it at a certain distance, and as history represents it to us. Nothing carried on by human instruments, but has its irregularities, and affords ground for criticism, when minutely scrutinized in matters of detail.[27]

Maisie Ward's chapter of **Young Mr. Newman**, "Dr. Hampden and the Dogmatic Principle" recognized that Hampden had put "his finger upon the fundamental weakness in Anglicanism."[28] When an argument moves from Scripture to reasoning to reasonings upon reasonings, "'there must be in fact a repeated revelation to authorize us to assert that this kind of conclusion represents to us some truth concerning God.'"[29]

Newman had not yet made this weakness the basis of his doubt, but less than a decade into the future he would "doubt whether there was any middle ground between the Roman Catholic Church and total scepticism."[30]

The Bampton Lectures of Hampden were at the foundation of this doubt. His intense work on his **Elucidations** between February 8th and 13th of 1836, Hampden's pamphlet came out on the former and Newman's on the latter date, led Newman to follow the argument closely.

States of Mind

States of mind alert us to an individual's position by questioning not only what position is held, but how and why that point of view is held. Not only did Newman always put himself into the minds of his beholders, but he consciously used states of mind as a rhetorical tool. In my work, then, I attempt to lead the reader into Newman's state of mind; and in so doing, I will be engaging the reader in a propaedeutic tool as well as instructing in possible uses of sophisticated rhetorical techniques.

Many possible definitions of state of mind abound, so it will be most important to be brief. It can be a habit of mind, as one individual may be speculative and dreamy, another may be sceptical and hesitant, still a third can have a distinctly philosophical habit of mind, pensive and equable.

State of mind can refer to temper. The ancient four-fold distinction of "humours," choleric, sanguine, phlegmatic, and melancholic, describe the basic temperaments of human. A person of melancholic temperament, like Hamlet, simply couldn't understand why a sanguine personality like Horatio would not let anything upset him. A modern description of personalities can be found in Jung, introversion, extroversion, thinking, feeling, intuition, perception, and so on.

State of mind can simply be the human awake state. It implies awareness, and a time element; that is, being aware of time, past, present, future, and chronology says something about human capabilities and perspectives. Such an awareness brings about an integrated perception of the present. The mind can focus its attention like directing a beam of light upon a single point, it makes its selection through time, and it is conscious of being molded by infinite variances and nuances changing throughout time. Thus one's point of view is not only today's perspective, but irrevocably some kind of totality of every day's perspective.

The state of mind is a function of knowing. The Sphinx asked a question. Numerous people tried to answer and failed. Oedipus approached the riddle not with superior intellect, but with a different function of knowing, a different means of formulating the parts of the riddle, a certain kind of wit.

Robert Henle, S.J., as dean of the graduate school at St. Louis University, was accustomed to summarize the changes which took place in the students during their programs as the development of a graduate habit of mind. In studying Newman's **Idea** and **Grammar**, I can well grasp where he obtained this custom. Newman wrote in the **Grammar**

> And, in fact, these three modes of entertaining propositions, doubting them, inferring them, assenting to them, are so distinct in their action, that, when they are severally carried out into the intellectual habits of an individual, they become the principles and notes of three distinct states or characters of mind.[31]

In the **Idea**, we realize that beyond acquirements are several ways of naming such states of mind as result from an education: enlargement of mind, enlightenment, philosophy, and such like. On the other hand, in **Callista**, a non-academic setting, we find that states of mind refer to a developing apprehension of the purpose of life with its direction towards God or away.

In its earliest stages, it is a state of doubt. In its ultimate stage, it is a state of certitude. In between it is an inquiry and once the final stage is achieved it is an investigation. Correspondingly, in **Loss and Gain**, an academic setting where states of mind are formed and forming, we find a movement towards views. These states of mind are sometimes prematurely possessed and hence become blocks to further questions; or these states of mind are characteristic positions of the different faiths available in Oxford at the time. Again, in the **Apologia**, Newman had not yet recognized the distinction he worked out in Chapters 4 and 6 of the **Grammar**, hence he confused the psychological experience of his movement towards assent and the variations of his inferences during this movement with the typical Humean and Lockean degrees of assent. His changing inferences contrasted with his continuing principle which he recognized in the **Apologia**: the same in 1833, 1845, and 1864.

The issues raised in his writings are carefully put forth in the series of 15 sermons preached before his audience at Oxford. The parallels become apparent in reviewing the definitions laid out in the preface of **Oxford University Sermons** where Newman made the assumptions of the **Grammar** evident. He did this before an audience which was open to his word with the publication of both the **Apologia** and the "Dream of Gerontius." Thus he could write: "For instance, in the case of Revealed Religion, according as one other of these is paramount within him,

> a man is a **sceptic** as regards it;
>
> or a **philosopher**, thinking it more or less
>
> > probably considered as a conclusion of
> >
> > reason,
>
> or he has an unhesitating faith in it,
>
> and is recognized as a **believer**.
>
> If he simply disbelieves, or **dissents**,
>
> > then he is assenting to the contradictory
> >
> > of the thesis (emphases added).
>
> Many minds of course there are, which are not
>
> under the predominant influence of any one of the
>
> > three.

Thus men are found to be irreflective, impulsive, unsettled, or again of acute minds,

> who do not know what they believe,
>
> and what they do not, and
>
> who may be by turns sceptics, inquirers,
>
> > or believers.

. . . Nay, further, in all minds there is certain co-existence of these distinct acts; that is, of two of them, for we can at once infer and assent."[32]

Thus we come to the fact that the term "states of mind," for which the **Oxford English Dictionary** gives numerous definitions had to be considered in light of the context of the writing. Yet in each case it is an indication of the fact that we are settling down to a habit of mind. This habit can be rooted in principle, or it can be the result of the ethos of our university, our company, or our religion. Newman spent himself to catch the particular states of mind of those about him because he was forever an apologist.

An interesting example, of Newman's way for entering into the inquirer's state of mind, which could be multiplied, is in Bertrand Russell's **Autobiography**: "Those who knew Whitehead well became aware of many things in him which did not appear in more casual contacts. . . . He was at all times deeply aware of the importance of religion. As a young man, he was all but converted to Roman Catholicism by the influence of Cardinal Newman."[33]

> A deep relation and a fundamental distinction exist between certainty and certitude. 'Certainty' is like an adjective, describing the trustworthiness, quality, level, value, mode of inference, kind of opinion, of a proposition. 'That Caesar once lived' has a certain measure of certainty. It can be tested, probed, adjusted, and reflected. A central feature of certainty is the quality of infinitely-shaded scales of certainty. But 'certitude' is not a quality of a proposition or a judgement. Strictly speaking, for Newman certitude has no contents, specifically, but it is an act of the mind upon making judgements. Certitude is the moving of the mind to accept what is before it, regardless of the precise character or nature of the certainty of the modes or propositions themselves. Certitude is the pronouncement of acceptance or rejection by the mind, sometimes fully informed of its results and processes, but not necessarily. When the judge pronounces the sentence, he assents that the defendant has guilt. The defendant has either guilt or he has not; the pronouncement does not fix the degree, but merely claims that it is so.[34]

Methods of Thought

In order to understand Newman, one must realize his methods of thought for deciding the significance of one's prejudices, biases, direction of thought, willingness to change, philosophy, theology, religion, art, rhetoric, and so on.

In his use of methods of thought, we will find the sharp dichotomy he felt between logic and rhetoric. Though he was able to assist Whately in writing the latter's logic, nonetheless Newman's **Grammar** makes it obvious that his preferences and talents were rhetorical rather than logical.

Newman sympathized with the many who object to logic and he understood those who enjoyed using it, but his position on how we reason went far beyond it. Thus he was especially proud of two of his discoveries: the method of thought he called **antecedent reasoning** and the faculty of thought he called the **illative sense**. The first is a shaping of experience which makes us amenable to certain principles and hypotheses. We assume and take for granted certain avenues of search because we have tendencies and mental sets which prepare us to see evidence and to fashion evidence in regard to the problems we possess an illative sense to face. And the illative sense is our faculty for moving to judgment. It is peculiar to our experience and preferences. Because the audience consists of those with states of mind and principles and methods of thought which are peculiar to each, Newman studied people in order to convince them and to persuade them to his way of judgment. As singular as our illative sense is, our states of mind, methods of thought, and principles are common. As a rhetorician, Newman respected the former and used the latter.

Newman sharply distinguished analysis and reasoning: logic and reasoning. A contrast between the significance of logic in the **Grammar** and the characteristic as reasoning make his method of thought obvious, e.g., explicit is found in

> clearness in argument
>
> accuracy in stating doctrines
>
> accuracy in stating principles
>
> not necessary to the integrity of the process analyzed
>
> but an account of (reasoning),
>
> not the cause of something being rational,
>
> not cause a given individual to reason better,

it does but give him

> a sustained consciousness, for good or for evil,
>
> > that he is reasoning.

"How a man reasons is as much a mystery as how he remembers."[35]

> Newman wrote on page 176 of the **Grammar**
>
> Even when argument is the most direct and severe
>
> of its kind, there must be
>
> those **assumptions** in the process which
>
> resolve themselves into the conditions of human nature;
>
> but how many more **assumptions**
>
> does that process in ordinary concrete matters involve,
>
> subtle **assumptions**
>
> not directly arising out of these primary conditions,
>
> but accompanying the course of reasoning,
>
> step by step,
>
> and traceable to the sentiments

of the age, country, religion, social habits and ideas,

of the particular inquirers or disputants,

and passing current without detection,

because admitted equally on all hands! . . .

Logic then does not really prove;

it enables us to join issue with others;

it suggests ideas;

it opens views;

it maps out for us the lines of thought;

it verifies negatively;

it determines when differences of opinion are hopeless; . . .

but for genuine proof in concrete matter

we require an **organon**

more delicate, versatile, and elastic

than verbal argumentation.

Newman did not rely on one single method, but on many, each accomplishing different ends. Houghton quoted: "'Such methods are antecedent probability, analogy, parallel case, testimony, and circumstantial evidences. . . .'" Newman mentioned other ways, such as the **ipse dixit** of authority, and explored his discovery of the illative sense.

Newman described the illative sense thoroughly in his **Grammar.** In the section "Natural Inference," he said "These are instances of a natural capacity, or of nature improved by practice and habit, enabling the mind to pass promptly from one set of facts to another, not only, I say, without conscious media, but without conscious antecedents."

He then wrote "This faculty, as it is actually found in us, proceeding from concrete to concrete, is attached to a definite subject-matter, according to the individual . . . a specific talent, and a ready exercise of it."

Thus principles, states of mind, and methods of thought are critical tools for understanding Newman. A good evaluation cannot be made of this subtle thinker without an appreciation for the manifold complexities of his art and ideas.

Why Principles?

I began my work on Newman by examining his principles. A Belgian, Iac Seynaeve, had earlier attempted to understand Newman through use of principles, but I felt that his work was unsatisfactory because the principles he chose were not actually Newman's; rather they were deductions Seynaeve fashioned.

A problem existed for us; Newman would state a principle, but he would not appear to adhere to it closely as one traced the principle through the text. Either Newman was inconsistent, unknowledgeable, or using different, albeit unspoken, criteria. Since we cannot accept the first two, we must look into the other criteria. Northrop Frye, in his **T. S. Eliot**, wrote that "Blake remarks that an intellectually honest man changes his opinions but not his principles, and this is so true of Eliot that it is possible to approach him deductively, treating the structure of his thought and imagery as a consistent unit."[36] And in Plato's **Meno**, Socrates says "Yes, Meno; but a principle which has any soundness would stand firm not only just now, but always."[37]

Why States of Mind and Methods of Thought?

At the same time I was reading Houghton. He said that Newman's state of mind changed throughout his work. If one could determine Newman's state of mind and the stimulus for writing, then one could ascertain Newman's method of thought. Charles Harrold agreed, but asked why Houghton had not followed up on his observation by giving many examples. Since my dissertation dealt with principles in Newman, I seized upon the idea of following up Houghton's insight and researching the framework of Newman's **organon** in detail.

Style

Walter Pater, Walter Houghton, and Herbert Read gave me tremendous insights into the entire body of Newman's work. Each one played a role in principles, states of mind, methods of thought, and style.

Walter Horatio Pater (1839 - 1894) was a critic, a humanist, literary author, and Oxford man. He wrote **Marius the Epicurean** in 1885. Although perhaps not well known as an author, Pater is respected as a critic, and his theory of Victorian prose is used by William E. Buckler in his book, **Prose of the Victorian Period.**

Pater's Victorian approach, utilized by Buckler, was summed up in a half dozen questions hidden in Pater's essay on style which Buckler raised in his Introduction:

1. Has the author taken a "full, rich, complex matter to grapple with?"

2. Has he achieved, in his language, balance between propriety and originality?

3. Has he provided for the reader an intense **intellectual** challenge?

4. Has he provided for the reader a worthwhile **formal** challenge?

5. Has he given to his prose work his own (or its own) unique personality?

6. Has he devoted his art to "great ends?"[38]

Charles Harrold wrote in his **English Prose of the Victorian Era**: "Victorian individuality is reflected in the variety of its prose: in the tortured and dynamic utterances of Carlyle; in the fine, flexible, intellectual prose of Newman; in the passionate though lucid eloquence of Ruskin; in the 'sinuous, easy, unpolemical' prose of Arnold; in the subtle, low-voiced, delicate rhythms of Pater. The work of these men is a splendid literary expression of their age, of its amazing energy and variety, and of its hopes, despairs, and ideals."[39]

"Had Newman been a less clear, less honest, less subtle thinker," Buckler wrote, "these two above named conditions would not have cooperated to make him the greatest Victorian prose stylist."

Rhythm

Pater wrote in an essay entitled "Style" in his book **Appreciations**,

> And prose thus asserting itself as the special
> and privileged artistic faculty of the present day,
> will be, however critics may try to narrow its scope,
> as varied in its excellence as humanity itself reflect-
> ing on the facts of its latest experience - an instru-
> ment of many stops, meditative, observant, descriptive,
> eloquent, analytic, plaintive, fervid. Its beauties
> will be not exclusively 'pedestrian:' it will exert,
> in due measure, all the varied charms of poetry, down
> to the rhythm which, as in Cicero, or Michelet, or Newman,
> at their best, gives its musical value to every
> syllable.[40]

Walter Houghton gave us examples of Newman's use of drama in **The Art of the Apologia**. Pater did not tell us why drama was natural to Newman, but he recognized that literature demanded organic style and that in light of his experience, Newman would use a dramatic style.

Extraversion and Introversion

Houghton saw that the extravert prefers thinking as exposition, the introvert prefers a narrative approach. J. S. Mill would stand for the former, a scientific and logical approach, as against Newman. Why is state of mind the prime question?

Surprisingly, Samuel Wilberforce provided Houghton the clue to the answer. Interestingly, Wilberforce was the one who continued on the Oxford Movement when Newman left for Catholicism. He was concerned to blunt the impact of Newman's secession from Anglicanism. When Newman's **Apologia** appeared, Wilberforce reviewed it in the **Quarterly Review** in a way Houghton appreciated. Wilberforce could make sense of Newman's journey on the basis of his introspective attitude and meaning. Houghton followed this lead, including the significant passages Wilberforce selected.

From his close analysis of these passages, Houghton knew that the unity of Newman's style came from his full acceptance of what it is to be introverted. Just as Wilberforce contrasted an extrovert, Athanasius, with Newman; so Houghton contrasted Mill with Newman. Reading the latter example in Houghton makes Wilberforce's case more convincing. Wilberforce held that Newman was sincere and extraordinarily open in the **Apologia**, but that his vacillation due to his intuitive introversion led him to leave the Anglican Church.

Wilberforce interpreted and evaluated the **Apologia** on the basis of an extroversion-introversion comparison. Athanasius, Newman's favorite Father of the Church, pursued an extroverted approach to the creed, cult, and code constitutive of the Church. Dogma was abstract and inflexible for this defender of orthodoxy against the Arians. Newman, on the other hand, pursued an introverted approach. Wilberforce wrote "He was taught to appreciate, and even to judge of, all external truth mainly in its ascertainable bearings on his own religious experience."[41] And later, "With the introvertive tendency which we have ascribed to him, was joined a more subtle and speculative intellect, and an ambitious temper."[42]

Houghton admitted his dependency on Wilberforce for the section on "Theories of Psychology," but he ignored the coincidence of selecting pp. 260-261 of the **Apologia** as his example of wavering - the most significant example Wilberforce used. On page 29 of **The Art,** Houghton showed how important methods of thought were for Newman and that there were two he built into his style: back-and-back and back-and-forth. Back-and-back involved a series of reasons, each bolstering the preceding. Back-and-forth meant a wavering between the pro and the con. The reason Houghton then added that states of mind were more important than methods of thought was that the former tipped the scale in a particular direction. For this reason, a Jungian analysis of Newman's prose similar to what Wilberforce and Houghton carried out makes sense.

Just as Houghton agreed that Newman's introverted tendency kept him open to a devious and nuanced consideration of the issues, so Herbert Read linked unity, imagination, and impressionism with such a tendency. Few were more obsessed with unity than Newman; as for imagination, he did not depend upon the external world for food for it, but found more than enough within himself; and clearly his expressionism fulfilled Read's definition of it as "visionary notion."

Read compared Walter Pater with Newman in order to bring out the difference of qualities. He wrote on page 183 of **English Prose Style:**

> Contrast them with the qualities of another writer whose style is equally integral and equally eloquent - I mean John Henry Newman. Newman's aim in writing was almost directly contrary to Pater's; he tells us . . .

that he has never written for writing's sake, but that
his one and single desire and aim had been 'to do what
is so difficult, viz., to explain clearly and exactly
my meaning; this has been the whole principle of all
my corrections and re-writings.' This eloquence that
is undeniably his, one of the most persuasive in English
literature, in the first instance owes little to conscious rhetoric or composition. It is a spirit, which
finds the modes of its eloquence inherent in its moods.
(As Craik wrote) 'Newman's style being in the lowest
terms an effort after a clear and exact representation
of his thought, it follows that not a little of the
fascination it exercises is the influence of the writer's
beautiful and subtle mind, which it clothes in light
and transparent vesture.'[43]

Yet Read did not select a specimen of Newman for his **English Prose Style**
because "Newman's passion is too subtle, and too little understood."

Read divided his work on the basis of the objective and the subjective
into a half on Composition and a half on Rhetoric. The rhetorical he divided
into eight chapters on the basis of Carl Jung's types which became styles
for Read. The table, found on p. 85, is as follows:

	EXTRAVERSION	**INTROVERSION**
Thinking	exposition	narrative
Feeling	fancy	imagination (invention)
Sensation	impressionism	expressionism
Intuition	eloquence	unity

The extraverted prefers the environment and the input from this source.
The introverted prefers the self and the input from within. Granted that
all of us are both extraverted and introverted, nonetheless we realize that
those of us who are introverted are better prepared for this century. The
introverted are aware of symbols and accept the vague; the extraverted are
explicit and taken up with the material. The insistent division into the
masculine and the feminine; into the Antiochean and Alexandrian; into the
Homeric epic and the Virgilian epic; into the left brain and the right brain;

into the logical and the rhetorical; into the scientific and the humanistic, as well as into the visual and the oral/aural; into the storyline and the removal of the storyline, was well captured by Walter Ong and Marshall McLuhan.

Oral Style

Because we have noted that Newman was a rhetorician, on the side of the feminine, Alexandrian, Virgilian, and the humanistic, it will come as no surprise that he is oral/aural. Gerard Manley Hopkins considered that Newman was an oral writer, and wrote to Coventry Patmore:

> When I read Newman's and some other modern writers, the same impression is borne in upon me: no matter how beautiful the thought, nor, taken singly, with what happiness expressed, you do not know what **writing prose** is. At bottom what you do and what Cardinal Newman does is to think aloud. . . . In this process there are certain advantages; they may outweigh those of a perfect technique; but at any rate they exclude that; they exclude the belonging technique, the belonging rhetoric, their own proper eloquence of written prose.[44]

Newman understood the validity of Hopkins' criticism of his writing style. He also appreciated the merit of Hopkins' admission that a conversational style could be higher than a written style. He captured Read's distinction between composition and rhetoric. Rhetoric is what Newman was all about, and yet to achieve his persuasive style, he had to be willing to endure great thought and great pains so that the reader would not think the work was "a great book (and) a great evil." And Read might well be right in finding Newman's reasons for forsaking a written style for an oral style in the latter's comments concerning Gibbon recorded in his **Autobiographical Writings.**

> With all his (Gibbon's) faults, his want of simplicity, his affectation, and his monotony, few can be put in comparison with him; and sometimes, when I reflect on his happy choice of expressions, his vigorous

> compression of ideas, and the life and significance
> of his every word, I am prompted indignantly to exclaim
> that no style is left for historians of an after day.[45]

In fact, Hopkins held that Newman lacked the essential for unity "the strain of address" - because he removed the storyline.[46] We must enter into the continuing conversation with him as we must with Joyce and Poe. We must give coherence to the unending parts. The public had a vague suspicion that Newman lacked simplicity and forthrightness. His exquisite care to use just the right word and his concern to push his statement of his understanding just as far as he held that it could or should be pushed was beyond the public. But Newman revealed his states of mind, his methods of thought, and his principles. Knowing these, his opponents and his readers today will have a critical way to approach him.

Read introduced excellent specimens of prose with a remarkable concern for the reader and the writer without self-consciousness. The eight divisions of his Jungian approach jibed with the eight divisions of rhetoric. Although Leonard Woolf could quibble on the exact match of these two sets of eight, he accepted the value of the approach and the value of the work for critics. He claimed that Read's **English Prose Style** merited acclaim on two counts: "It is intelligent and it is impersonal."[47] Similarly, Newman could consider himself in the third person as he could consider his closest friends.

Woolf admired Read's objectivity, writing "What a relief it is to find a critic like Mr. Read, who, for a whole book, can forget that he is himself a writer and thus can devote himself impersonally to the pursuit of truth."[48] This high praise prepared the reader for a difficult reading. A like disinterestedness was expected from the reader. In return one would learn of composition and style. Woolf complained that this term was really inadequate for what Read had in mind. In fact, "their value depends upon the fact that his classification is based upon a subtle and sensitive analysis of the psychology of literary composition. The various styles are, in his view, the result of the combination in the writer's mind of Logic, Speculation, Emotion, or Character with either Thought or Sensibility."[49]

Whereas Read applied his division to a number of great prose writers, the present work limits itself to Newman. Since Newman was an extreme introvert, it is only necessary to use the four divisions of the introvert explicitly; but since Jung recognized that there is always a shadow, the extraverted divisions are also present. Indeed, Newman himself recognized that in order to appeal to extraverted readers he would have to fashion explicit examples and concrete illustrations within his abstract and imaginative reasoning.

Writings

With Read's Jungian approach and Pater's Victorian approach, we can develop a specimen type theory for Newman on the basis of his writings. The three major works which deserve to be more widely read in our own age are **Apologia Pro Vita Sua, The Idea of a University,** and **An Essay in Aid of a Grammar of Assent.** But in order to understand Newman fully, and to appreciate the ongoing processes in his three masterpieces, we should investigate among other writings **Loss and Gain, Callista, a Tale of the Fourth Century, The Oxford University Sermons,** and **An Essay on the Development of Christian Doctrine.** In addition, other sources will be called upon to assist us in our search: "The Second Spring," "Dream of Gerontius," "Lead, Kindly Light," **Letters and Diaries of John Henry Newman,** and various other sermons and writings. A complete bibliography appears at the end of this work.

Apologia as a Starting Point

A final word. An introduction or a preface, as a critic put it, is meant to improve the reader's pursuit of truth just as the rules of rhetoric and grammar are meant to assure the reader's accuracy in carrying out this pursuit. Each age has an impact upon its writers. Crucial to this impact is the sensory, psychological, educational, and cultural context within which the author writes, but equally, within which the audience reads or listens. The complexity of the Victorian Age requires a corresponding complexity of contexts on the part of the reader or listener despite the necessary commonness of the age. The best way to see this may well be to examine John Henry Newman's prose.

But the trickiest thing is to catch on to "anxieties and deliverances" in Newman. The **Apologia** gave Newman many anxieties because he was not certain how he could prove that he honestly held one belief, one set of principles throughout his career. Newman forthrightly explained himself, but he recognized many did not find him clear. So he dissected his thoughts and language in the **Grammar**.

So often throughout Newman's life and writings we find references to loss, anxiety, illness, wandering, sea storms. Newman finds his way to safe harbor, fuller understanding, and faith. When he has gained himself, he can accept the loss with equanimity. But before he can gain, he must lose. Before he can understand, he must go through the **after**, that is, after he has gone through the whole, the beginning makes sense. I had been using the **Grammar** and the **Idea** in my classes for several years. I began to notice that the better students would read the **Apologia** on their own to get a better understanding of the two texts used in class. Only after they went through the whole thing in their minds again did they experience that fuller understanding of Newman, and why he took the subtle, nuanced path he had. They really understood Newman only after they had finished what they had been through before.

THE IDEA OF A UNIVERSITY WITH TEST CASES

Introduction to Principle

Newman's use of principle and its effectiveness are evident from the following specimens and comments of his critics.

> Science, then, has to do with things, literature with thoughts; science is universal, literature is personal, but literature uses language, science uses words merely as symbols, but literature uses language in its full compass, as including phraseology, idiom, style, composition, rhythm, eloquence, and whatever other properties are included in it.

> Let us then put aside the scientific use of words, when we are to speak of language and literature. Literature is the personal use or exercise of language. That this is so is further proved from the fact that one author uses it differently from another. Language itself in its very origination would seem to be traceable to individuals. Their peculiarities have given it its character. We are often able, in fact, to trace particular phrases or idioms to individuals. We know the history of their rise.[1]

Literature

The method of thought which is evident through this lecture is that of contrast. In order to keep his audience involved, Newman criticized a leading critic, Sterne. He used his inadequate positions to bring out the contrast he noted between science and literature. Sterne had ignored the unity of thought and writing; thus he had ignored the key difference Newman would stress - the personal. Science dealing with things is impersonal. Literature dealing with thoughts is personal. For this reason, style and writing go together. To make this point more concretely, Newman considered the thought of those who distinguished and separated thought and style, as if style were an addition.

Specimens: Digression on Dangers

The danger in the use of specimens is that we will generalize, that we will assume we have covered the whole of Newman. Nedoncelle reminds us that to understand anything of Newman we must read all of his writings. Powell warns us of the danger of reductionism. To make this danger clearer, let us consider Gilbert Garraghan's **Literature of Cardinal Newman**.

> It is in this connection that Newman's literary methods are particularly instructive. His cast of mind was unique in its union of profound sensibility with the severest logic. He was a poet, but he was also a close and careful thinker. Hence, clearness, sequence, orderly arrangement, adequacy of treatment characterize his writings; in a word, they are strong in all the elements that enter into the notion of rhetorical structure.[2]

Yet Muriel Spark claimed in **Selected Letters** that Newman was incoherent.[3]

How can we reconcile this? By considering the genre, the purpose, the state of mind, and the method of thought Newman was using at the time of the writing and in his many revisions. An 1858 lecture is something which we could expect to be clear, orderly, and adequate to its purpose; but this purpose sets limits - how much more could Newman have said on literature.

Here he is attempting a definition which by its nature means limits. On the other hand, the **Apologia** is a rushed work; the **Grammar** is ordered but it is a set of specimens, as is clear from its conclusion; his definitions of assent are not taken up once more upon carrying out the development of certitude; nor after taking up what the difference of assent and inference is. The **Via Media** is attacked by the preface to the 3rd edition. The rambling **Loss and Gain** is not corrected. The **Apologia** is cut by one hundred pages immediately upon its publication in 1864. This 1865 edition is towards a distant and disinterested audience; as the 1864 was towards a contemporaneous and interested audience.

Newman knew that his friends would object: "Nor is it the least part of my trial, to anticipate that, upon first reading what I have written, my friends may consider much in it irrelevant to my purpose; yet I cannot help thinking that viewed as a whole, it will effect what I propose to myself in giving it to the public."[4]

It is important to remember that Newman could be passionate. When he retorted in 1862 that he was not returning to the Anglican Church, his language was almost incoherent. Only his modesty and humility kept it within bounds. And in 1864, he was passionate in his defense; in his apology. The order and the language were not apo*logetic, but apologe*tic.

> A certain degree of passion is to be found in a writer like Walter Pater. . . . But how to describe this inner unity, in Pater's case? It is a subtle matter, and some have doubted if anything more considerable than just a self-consuming passion for style, and educated taste, an abnormal sensibility for the tonal value of words, could be deduced. These qualities are not to be despised, but contrast them with the qualities of another writer whose style is equally integral and equally eloquent I mean John Henry Newman.
>
> Newman's aim in writing was almost directly contrary to Pater's; he tells us (in Letter, II. 477, quoted by Canon Beeching in Craik's **English Prose**, v. 444) that he has never written for writing's sake, but that his one and single desire and aim had been 'to do what is difficult, viz., to explain clearly and exactly my meaning; this has been the whole principle of all my corrections and re-writings.' The eloquence that is undeniably his, one of the most persuasive in English.[5]

"LITERATURE" from the **Idea**

Gilbert Garraghan had two purposes in writing **Literature: Cardinal Newman**: "to introduce the student to the critical analysis of a prose style of acknowledged excellence and to serve him as a starting point in his acquisition of a body of sound principle and theory regarding literature and its problems."[6] This present work could well have had those two purposes and started with this same lecture following the lead of Garraghan and another outstanding critic, Walter Pater, who depended upon this lecture for his own theory which he gave us in **Appreciations**; but even though this work has resulted from a different starting point: **Callista**; nonetheless for the reader's sake in revamping the order of the parts, this work has been selected as the starting point.

Principle of the Mean

In this work, Newman's use of principle and the effectiveness of this use are most evident. From its introduction to its conclusion this use is consistent. His first principle is that contained in the marvelous digression in Plato's **Statesman**: art achieves its end by searching out that which is an evil - the excess and the defect. Art requires the mean; to be neither too much nor too little. And Newman in his opening sentence put it similarly: "I tried to find a subject for discussion, which might be at once suitable to the occasion, yet neither too large for your time, nor too minute or abstruse for your attention."

Principle of Discrimination

Later we will see this principle in a Discourse from the **Idea** and this lecture laid out with sufficient white space to make the clarity of the argument and the principle equal to the physical arrangement, but for now we will continue to the second principle: eloquence often masks "a mixture of truth and falsehood, which it will be my business to discriminate from each other." In the lecture, "Christianity and Scientific Investigation," Newman claimed that the purpose of a university is to discriminate. Here he gives the basis for this. Whenever we write we have a mixture of truth and falsehood which the reader is responsible to distinguish. Thus an essay is to begin with the challenge of an **aporia**. What is the common experience bolstered by the leaders of society? This must be questioned in order that we might separate the truth from the falsehood.

Principle of Literature as a Personal Work

Though we are accustomed to consider literature as a written work and the results of cooperation among many, Newman had an insight into the fact that the oral precedes the written. As Walter Ong has argued at length in **Orality and Literacy**, we have been structured in our thinking and hence in our acting by various forms of writing from the time of the Greeks to the word processor, nonetheless prior to this is either the primary orality of certain groups or the secondary of our literate group. From a consideration of the personal aspect of the spoken word, Newman goes on to the contrasting experience of science and its manner of dealing with things by means of symbols. The farther removed the scientist is from the personal and the spoken, the more fully scientific he or she is.

Principle of the Unity of Thought and Speech

Flowing from the personal principle is that of the unity of thought and speech. "Matter and expression are parts of one; style is a thinking out into language." In order to make this obvious, Newman contrasted the options one would grasp at to separate thought and speech: making it a **thing**, making it a mere verbal symbol, making it a case of mere words. Each of these attempts at separation collapses in light of the fact that literature is truly "thoughts expressed in language."

What are the results of these principles? These principles rebut the charges of the critic. Newman had taken Lawrence Sterne as his foil since this outstanding novelist and writer of sermons had presented three clear **aporiae** in one section of a single sermon. Newman could thus find his needed objections in a handy form by an extremely well known author of the highest reputation in the two most important areas of literature at that time: secular and religious. Thus before coming to Shakespeare and Cicero, Newman had used the principles. Then he entered into the objections in the concrete. "Since the thoughts and reasonings of an author have, . . . a personal character, no wonder that his style is not only the image of his subject, but of his mind." Twice he exemplified Shakespeare, once from "Macbeth" and once from "Hamlet." In each, he showed the genius of the Bard overflowing into "a many-membered period."

Principle of the Elaborate

With these two authors, Newman found the means to rebut Sterne's claim that authors are redundant and studied. Instead, using the principle of the personal style as a shadow of the writer, Newman demonstrated that an abundance of members fitted the fullness of the mind of the author. In order to clinch his argument against the charge of elaborateness, he compared the patterns of the painter and the sculptor. These use studios, not to become studied in their work, but to have an opportunity to work over their creations until they would meet their standard of perfection.

A writer is not to be upbraided if he or she "should pause, write, erase, rewrite, amend, complete, before he satisfies himself that his language has done justice to the conceptions which his mind's eye contemplated."

Principles of Rhetoric

Once Newman had answered the objections which Sterne's sermon had
offered, he exhibited, in the last two sections of the lecture, the principles of rhetoric which teachers of literature in his university would
be teaching. In section 9 he summed up the essay and in section 10 he
gave his conclusion. "Literature, then, is of a personal character; it
consists in the enunciations and teachings of those who have a right to
speak as representatives of their kind, and in whose words their brethren
find an interpretation of their own sentiments, a record of their own experience, and a suggestion for their judgments." "It will not answer to make
light of literature or to neglect its study; rather we may be sure that,
in proportion as we master it in whatever language and imbibe its spirit,
we shall ourselves became in our own measure the ministers of like benefits
to others, be they many or few, be they in the obscurer or the more distinguished walks of life, who are united to us by social ties and are within
the sphere of our personal influence." In concluding this work with encouragement to those who would be responsible for this area of knowledge, Newman
showed his awareness of the importance of persuasion for a rhetorician
and in summarizing the topic through the use of the last two words - "personal influence" - he proved how complete his awareness was.

Though the present work is concerned with much more than principles,
it is necessary to begin with these in order that the readers will appreciate
the basis for agreement or disagreement with the argument. Newman noted
that most arguments which turn into controversy do so either because the
participants do not understand one another's vocabulary or meanings or
they differ in principle. If the latter, there is no way to salvage the
dispute, but it also shows it to be vain; while in the former case it is

only necessary to clarify what are the meanings.

In this first chapter, the search for principles was accomplished without copious quotations from Newman's work. In future chapters where the rhythm, structure, states of mind, and methods of thought are searched for it will be incumbent to use a more detailed specimen approach. These specimens will be instances where both the uniqueness and the commonness of the subject have been taken into account.

The danger in the use of specimens is that we will generalize, that we will assume we have covered the whole of Newman, as we noted above.

Nicholas Lash is clear, in introducing the University of Notre Dame edition of the **Grammar**, on why it is difficult to analyze Newman or to criticize him. He always grasps the whole and approaches it from many vantage points. This is especially obvious in the **Idea** where he usually divided a discourse into 10 sections. Yet only through such a convergence did Newman expect to share his view with others. As a rhetorician he took into account the many objections his audience contained and developed a counter argument for each. This often would lead the less disciplined reader to miss the point of his argument, while for the disciplined it provided a panorama of the issues involved in a subtle and complex issue. Once another had the opportunity to take the same view, or achieve the same state of mind as Newman, his work was completed, since he did not expect to force his opponent to accept his principle from the mere weight of an argument. Rather than to force, he would only share as fully as possible what had been sufficiently persuasive to him. The temptation of one who desired to analyze Newman was to assume in practice that he had a system. Despite the fact that these authors explicitly state that Newman is not systematic, they nonetheless pursue his thought as if it were systematic. Newman himself not only in the **Grammar** but in other writings exposed the dislike he had for system, so much so that he was forced at times to make his own position seem ridiculous. However, a rhetorical approach to Newman enables us to avoid making too much of his inconsistency and of his seeming excessive stand against system. This habit indicates how fully Newman was on the side of Samuel Coleridge in the Bentham/Coleridge distinction which James Stuart Mill outlined so convincingly in his **Autobiography**.[7] Yet this lack of system seems belied by the exceptional use of a visual approach to his rhetoric which is perfectly exemplified in the opening of the third volume of **Historical Sketches** which follows in the form of a digression and a link.

Historical Sketches

A help in grasping the value of the visual approach of Newman is in **Historical Sketches**. Newman considered discipline and influence at the level of principle in answering the question: What is a university? And he answered the question in light of the meaning of a world. A world is a personal reality. A reality whose unity is in its interests. Only where interests are adequate will we find a world. We find a world where our aims are exceptional and lasting.

Beyond our aims are our methods. Through the ages our methods for achieving a bond powerful enough to constitute a world are personal. Person-to-person sharing of our interests in a common area guarantees the continuation of our world.

His use of these elements of definition result in a principle, but once the principle is clear we can turn the order of his sketch about. We can begin with the contrast between books and the voice. In pursuit of the basics of a discipline we can do it as well at home. In pursuit of the life of a discipline we can not do it as well at home, we need the personal influence of others. This is his principle.

Originally we can go back to the point made by Aristotle that a community can be as large as the throng to which the voice can reach. Our worlds were limited to such smaller communities of interest. This assumption Newman expanded in considering the issue and the principle. He contrasted "You may learn" with "You must catch," as he balanced "makes it live in us" with "in whom it lives already." This method of thought has a rhythm to it. We feel the need to leave home and carry out a pilgrimage to a university.

We feel this because just prior to this principle, Newman had divided his definition in two: a) our highest aims and b) our ancient method of teaching orally. Here, too, Newman stressed the principle of unity. When we combine such aims and methods, we have the basis for a world. Our common interests mutually shared not only provide the nature of a world, but of the variety of worlds we can choose to join. Because this article is the first in the third volume of the **Historical Sketches** and because Newman used this method of thought to change the state of mind he labeled Public Opinion, he put a great effort into its rhetoric. Both the rhythm and the structure unite to give it a power for any audience, but especially for one interested in the number of worlds he highlighted to reveal his principle.

"The general principles of any study you may learn by
books at home;

     but the detail, the colour, the tone, the air,

       the life which makes   it live in us,

       you must catch

     all these from those in whom it lives already.

     Whenever men are really serious about getting . . .

'a good article,'

when they aim at   something refined

something really luminous,

something really large,

something choice, they go to another market;

they avail themselves, in some shape or other,

of a visual method,

the ancient method,

of oral instruction,

of present communication between man and man,

of teachers instead of learning,

of the personal influence of a master,

and the humble initiation of a disciple,

and in consequence,

of great centres of pilgrimage and thong,

which such a method of education

necessarily involves.

This, I think, will be found to hold good in all those departments
or aspects of society, which possess an interest sufficient to bind men
together, or

to constitute what is called 'a world.'

It holds   in the political world, and

in the high world, and

in the religious world; and

it holds also

in the literary and scientific world."

Test Case: Idea

This work has stressed the significance of states of mind and antecedent reasoning. A test case for the reader is to examine the relations of **idea** in Newman as others have done in Coleridge. The starting point for such an examination is in how state of mind and idea relate to image. When he developed the **Grammar**, he considered the Thought, the Idea, the Image, and the Mediation of Christ. He could have used what he had learned from Aquinas on the relation of the Father and the Son as Thought, Image, and Idea. But instead he used the idea as he had in the **Idea of a University**. This idea went back to the forms of Plato, back to Origen, back to the insights of Coleridge, and back to his own work on Development.

The principle of origin is at the base of this. A principle or a cause brings something into existence. The likeness is similar to the principle, but only at its maturity. When we bring forth a child it is originally not too much like ourselves, but certain aspects of it are apparent. These show the direction; the aim; the objective; the goal. We must care for the idea. It is vulnerable to monstrosity and fragility, as **The Phenomenon of Man** argued. He showed how we move from step to step by thresholds and boiling so that a new form comes about. The idea is also vulnerable to the many changes of the cultures and the ages. Each age has its own **scientia**. We are vulnerable to methods and techniques of each age. We go through a series of changes, keeping something of the best of the past.

Time works out the confusion, the contrarieties, the contradictions. We use our imaginations on different instances. Each instance rests in our memories, in our judgments. We judge and we retain something of the result. Our actions suddenly achieve a meaning and we are converted. Our conversion is our reversal upon discovery. Unless we search we do not change nor discover. Yet the ultimate faith is beyond us. We cannot atone for ourselves; we must depend upon Christ for his mediation. We accept our sinfulness, our failure, our past life, and our social learning from all who have gone before us.

This is passed on by word and deed, by monument and oral tradition. We look at the past through the future. Where is this going? We doubt ourselves; we doubt mankind; if we know God we cannot doubt Him. Our faith is towards Him, but so much of past experience is recorded; this record reminds us to continue our search so we can be witnesses for a future generation. Each similarity and difference offers us something to share, something of the idea.

Idea is a conception; a growth; a birth; a revelation; a continuation; a fulfillment; a nucleus of meaning; a tradition; an image; a mandala; a link between the past and the future; a challenge; a reward; a need; a basis for freedom; a part of a whole; a whole with its parts; an **imago Dei**.

As the Son is like the Father; as the Word is of the Truth, Primal Truth, so anything and any knowledge is an image of the Father. We prize His Glory in the gift of his word. Each Idea is a reflection of the Truth, the **Vera Prima**.

In the specimen from Pusey, we have an example of states of mind and principle. This famous introduction had the lovers of the **Apologia** as its chief audience; therefore the next chapter will be on integrity of mind in these two works. Before that we will have two test cases.

Test Case: Tamworth Reading Room

An interesting test case for the question of style arises from a consideration of the Tamworth letters and the **Oxford University Sermons** - the context of the Tamworth letters compared with the context of **Oxford University Sermons.** Newman had heard of Lord Brougham on how it could be possible to achieve the moral education of the poor by museums and libraries. When he heard Robert Peel's reiteration of this proposal, Newman decided to satirize the latter. To do this, he played upon the comparison of the limitations of the two.

If Brougham so little distinguished between moral and intellectual objectives of education, he showed himself a fool. Yet Peel imitated his foolish approach. How much less than his master was Peel, who could not be original in his buffoonery. This style fitted the newspaper where the Tamworth letters were first published. It little fitted the **Idea.** Nonetheless Newman wanted to use the material.

He changed the style by separating himself from the state of mind of himself as its author. Years after he could look upon that previous state of mind as that of another. An objective statement of the original satire could now find its place in a serious work. Brougham was dead. Peel was dead. No longer did Newman have to write anonymously. Instead he could reveal his state of mind as one exonerated of the charge that he was against the poor and against the masses. "Education is a high word; it is the preparation for knowledge, and it is the imparting of knowledge in proportion to that preparation."[8]

Newman can do little with a variety of audiences directly, but he can indirectly, by changing his own state of mind. The sense comes through in his **Apologia.**

His original state of mind is apologetic - but in his revision his later state of mind is autobiographical without the apologetic. Just as in the **Idea** where Newman faced an unknown audience so in the **Apologia's** version, he faced the audience of the future and no longer had to defend himself against Kingsley, instead he could be himself. Likewise in this reworking of his original attack upon Peel he could make the assumptions of the satire. Newman hoped the audience would recognize the imitation obvious in Peel's proposal. They would revert to the pompous concern of Brougham. In this argument, Newman would not have to show each weakness. He could let the experience of the English public since Brougham weigh Peel's proposal. If Brougham the master failed, how much more severely would Peel fail. Whereas we could expect for Peel that a "bad speaker" such as Brougham would prepare the way for his good speaking, Peel would mirror the past, positively and symbolically. Instead Newman made it clear that the mirror did not turn the bad speaker around, but brought out fully the limitations of non-educative approach.

Education is a voice. Not a museum. Not a book. Brougham lowered it to a common level. While an encyclopedia collects the common knowledge for the young, Brougham and Peel wanted to provide a means to the moral conduct of the poor. Neither showed any link between knowing and doing. Neither faced the limits of passion and evil. The assumption of grace which they ignored came out in Catholicus Clericus, a title for his anonymity. An Anglican Catholic Cleric would be aware of original sin and evil. Education by avoiding these would be doomed.

In his discourse, Newman could assume his audience was aware of the earlier contest with Brougham and Peel. His audience would know his changed state of mind in the **Idea**. His use of a changed method of thought. His new principle. If this were not the case, it was the fault of the audience which had the tools to know these changed aspects of his style. A later audience, after Walter Pater had extolled the **Idea** as the exemplar, would be in an even better situation to catch these.

Analogous to the Tamworth change is the **Oxford University Sermons** change. When Newman preached before the University as an Anglican and a fellow of Oxford, he searched for the relation between faith and reason. Through six sections of the XIVth Sermon he used the method of thought of comparison. Faith was between wisdom and reason. "I . . . inquire into the nature of Christian wisdom as a habit or faculty of mind distinct from Faith, the mature fruit of Reason and nearly answering to what is meant by philosophy, it must not be supposed that I am denying its spiritual nature or its divine origin."9

"Almighty God influences us and works in us

through our minds,

not without them or in spite of them;

as at the fall

we did not become other beings than

we had been,

but forfeited gifts

which had been added to us on our creation,

so under the Gospel

we do not lose any part of the nature in which

we are born,

but regain what we have lost.

We are what

we were,

and something more,

And what is true of God's dealings with our minds generally,

is true in particular as regards our reasoning power,

His grace does not supersede,

    but uses them, and

        renews them by using.

We gain truth by reasoning . . . in a state of nature:

We gain it in the same way in a state of grace."[10]

In this we recognize the rhythm Newman achieved. In this, we recognize the structure Newman developed. Moving the method of thought from reason in conjunction with faith and wisdom to philosophy, Newman found he could use the same approach but with a different state of mind - instead of a state of mind which depended upon faith and Almighty God, a state of mind in accordance with a state of nature. Thus in the **Idea** he argued that such a state of nature is open to more than nature.

Though Newman considered the need for the pro and the con in the sermon to be explicitly laid out, in the **Idea** this need no longer existed. Rather Newman let discrimination to the reader's powers. Whereas the original effort was for a time, as he showed in the previous sermon, beyond him, he had found a method of thought equal to the analysis he could make the issue clear enough for the English mind. "The process of the Reasoning Faculty is either explicit or implicit; that is, either with or without a direct recognition the part of the mind,

    of the starting point and

        path of thought from and

            through which it comes to its conclusion.

The process of reasoning, whether implicit or explicit,

    is the act of one and the same faculty,

  to which belongs the power of analyzing that process,

    and of thereby passing from implicit to explicit."[11]

Introduction for Younger Readers: Durkin

As the United States was to enter the Great Depression, Mary Durkin published **Introductory Studies in Newman: with Introduction, Notes, and Inductive Questions.** Her purpose was to keep the value of his writing before the young; hence she selected works which they would appreciate: historical sketches found in his sermons and fiction. The former include Saul, David, Augustine, Chrysostom, and Paul, while the latter include **Callista** and the **Dream of Gerontius.** Significantly, she chose the section on marriage and the description of the locust plague from the former and all of the dramatic poem.

Her introduction reveals the reputation Newman held at that time among educated Catholics: "Every one claiming to be an English scholar shall be familiar with the great Cardinal as a writer and know something of the vitality of his thought and the charm of his style."[12]

Beyond his thought and his style, Durkin found human interest, and by selecting these biographical and autobiographical specimens, she revealed a state of mind which is most appealing. Whereas Newman provided the positive and the negative in his **Apologia,** she found his use of exemplars gave Newman at his best. When the young would go on to other writings of Newman they could well wonder why he was such a controversialist and why he roused such controversy.

She had been fully persuaded by Newman and personal influence was her message also: "Cardinal Newman undoubtedly made use of every opportunity of influencing others. . . . To him the most momentous experience is that which personal beings gave of one another. In comparison with personal things all else is valueless."[13]

Two purposes offered criteria for her selections: the broadening and deepening of experience and the increase of ideals within the young. Her expectation was also twofold: that personal experiences would cause the young to become involved and reading of this type of Newman literature would prepare the way for a deeper reading. These purposes and expectations remind one of Whyte who took the opposite bent: the reader was to begin with Newman's work "Literature," and arrive at an either/or juncture: this is of such worth that one would continue, or one would reject any more of Newman. Because Whyte rejected Newman's principles, while accepting his style, he is in stark contrast with Durkin, but a necessary balance.

As persuasive as Newman can be, even his failure offers a sincerity and a style worthy of study. Hence as Charles Lyell could tell William Froude that the scientific community was moved by Newman's **Apologia** to the point that even though they would not accept his view they were eager to hear it, even in his failure such a writer is obviously one to be examined carefully.

In Discourse VII, Newman contrasted the option of a person who would have to learn something of everything with a person who was left without a tutor.

The principle which is at the heart of the **Idea** is that of liberal knowledge. Here Newman is following Aristotle: "Of possessions . . . those rather are useful, bear fruit, those liberal, which yield revenue

by fruitful, I mean, which yield revenue

by enjoyable, where nothing accrues of consequence beyond

the using."

"Why this distinction?

because that alone is liberal knowledge

which stands on its own pretensions,

which is independent of sequel,

    expects no complement,

    refuses to be **informed** by any end,

        or absorbed into any art,

in order to present itself to our contemplation duly.

The most ordinary pursuits have this specific character,

    if they are self-sufficient and complete;

the highest lose it,

    when they minister to something beyond them.

"Liberal" as applied to Knowledge

                and Education

expresses a specific idea,

which ever has been,

and ever will be,

while the nature of man is the same,

just as the idea of the Beautiful is specific

      or   of the Sublime,

      or   of the Ridiculous,

      or   of the Sordid.

continuous historical tradition

now

then

and

never out of the world.

There indeed have been differences of opinion on what constitutes the **Idea**. Here Newman shows the difference to make the point.

difference,

variation,

yes, same,

years,

Subjects vary with the age,

it varies not itself.

That idea must have substance in it

Variations imply the archetypal idea,

instead of discrediting it.

*

All things NOW are to be learned at once,

not first one thing, then another,

not one well,

but many badly.

Learning is to be

    without exertion,

    without attention,

    without toil;

    without grounding,

    without advance,

    without finishing.

There is nothing

to be nothing individual in it

the wonder of the age

act mechanically

passively

almost unconsciously

mere multiplication and

dissemination of volumes.

In contrast, as a method of thought, Newman brings out the positive nature of Education. This dissonance in preparation readies the reader's state of mind for his conclusion. Obviously, antecedent reasoning and a correct state of mind are not only integral to Newman's method of thought but to his view of Education. Hence he is correct in his claim that he was always an educator. His stress upon influence comes out here.

Education is a high word; it is the preparation for

knowledge

and it is the imparting of knowledge in

proportion to that preparation.

A University is

an Alma Mater,

knowing her children one by one,

not a foundry,

or a mint,

or a treadmill.

What was Newman's estimation of Julian the Apostate's state of mind and how did he use this in his method of thought? At the heart of Discourse VIII, Knowledge Viewed in Relation to Religion, Newman contrasted the proud and the amiable specimens of those who lead a spurious religion.

Page 146:

Such is the

final exhibition of the Religion of Reason:

in the insensibility of conscience,

in the ignorance of the very idea of sin,

in the contemplation of his own moral consistency,

in the simple absence of fear,

in the cloudless self-confidence,

in the serene self-possession,

in the cold self-satisfaction, we recognize the mere

Philosopher.

Why is this?

because they think and act as if there were really nothing

objective in their religion;

it is because conscience to them is not the rod of a lawgiver,

as it ought to be,

but the dictate of their own minds and nothing more;

it is because they do not look out of themselves,

because they do not look through and

beyond their own minds to their

Maker,

but are engrossed in notions of what is due to themselves,

to their own

dignity,

their own

consistency.

Julian was the exemplar of the mere Philosopher. Newman made concrete in Julian rather than in Socrates the limits of reason. This was apt since those Anglicans who would receive his message argued for the religion of Antiquity from which Julian became an apostate. The argument, which is still with us, that moral behavior is more important than religious belief had to be challenged. A concrete exposition of the state of mind of a person who exhibited imitable behavior provided a method of thought destined to persuade many who were unable to make subtle distinctions.   In Discourse VI Newman had etched such a state of mind:

(Knowledge viewed in relation to Learning)

"Intellect, which has been disciplined to the perfection of
its powers,

> which knows, and thinks while it know,

> which has learned to leaven the dense mass of

facts and events with the elastic force of reason,

> such an intellect cannot   be partial,

> > cannot   be exclusive,

> > cannot   be impetuous,

> > cannot   be at a loss,

> > cannot but be patient,

collected, and majestically calm

because it discerns the end in every beginning,

 the origin in every end,

 the law in every interruption,

 the limit in each delay;

because it ever knows where it stands,

and how its path lies from one to the other."[14]

Conclusion of the Idea

"That perfection of the Intellect, which is the result of Education,

> > and its **beau ideal**

to be imparted to individuals in their respective measures,

is the

> clear, calm, accurate vision

and comprehension of all things, as far as

the finite mind can embrace them,

each in its place,

and with its own characteristics upon it.

It is ALMOST prophetic from its knowledge of history;

it is ALMOST heart-searching from its knowledge of human nature;

it has ALMOST supernatural charity from its freedom from littleness and

prejudice;

it has ALMOST the repose of faith, because nothing can startle it;

it has ALMOST the beauty and harmony of heavenly contemplation, so intimate

is it with the eternal order of things

and the music of the spheres."[15]

In the middle of "Knowledge Viewed in Relation to Learning," Newman achieved the definition of the **Idea**. At the moment of this achievement he is concerned that his audience grasp the significance of what he had accomplished. Before there was only an inadequate appreciation of the meaning of education in its intellectual aspect. Newman must be elaborate to secure the attention and the comprehension of the audience.

Test Case: A Genealogy of Morals

"From Clapham to Bloomsbury"[16] by Gertrude Himmelfarb is an excellent test case for Bernard Lonergan's specimen of Newman's **Idea of a University**. Lonergan accepted McGrath's discovery of Newman's axiom on the place of religion in a university: religion is a form of knowledge; its removal distorts other forms of knowledge. With his acceptance of this **status quaestionis,** Lonergan confessed he could go no further. The history of the university in our century has been one of the removal of theology from the circle of studies: has the distortion taken place? Are we worse off for its absence?

Himmelfarb claims we are and she depends upon Newman's outstanding critic's biographer for her facts.

Noel Annan had written a life of Leslie Stephen in 1951; with the opening of the documents after the 75 year moratorium, he felt compelled to put out a second edition in 1984.

Leslie himself slipped from the Christian faith between 1859 and 1864. Annan claimed that "Aware though he was of the power of metaphysical systems over men's minds, Stephen believed too fundamentally in the March of Mind, the gradual elimination of error and folly in the light of new knowledge, for him to grasp how deeply, in fact, traditional morality was sustained by metaphysics."[17]

Himmelfarb carried an acceptance of this limitation even further in those whose ancestors had followed the Evangelical tradition, "Vanessa, Virginia, and Adrian Stephen . . ., Clive Bell (married to Vanessa), Maynard Keynes, Lytton Strachey, Duncan Grant, Desmond McCarthey, Roger Fry, and Saxon Sydney-Turner" had taken as their "credo: living for 'ourselves.'"[18] They took from G. E. Moore

> . . . a philosophy that sanctioned, if not immorality, then at the very least amorality. For the 'states of consciousness' that were at the heart of that philosophy had nothing to do with conduct or consequences. 'Being good' was their objective, not 'doing good.' And being good was being in those heightened states of consciousness, those 'timeless, passionate states of contemplation and communion' which were conducive to 'love, beauty, and truth' not virtue.[19]

No wonder then that our view of Victorian religion and morality has been so far from the mark. And that Himmelfarb can conclude with "We may also better appreciate the force of Nietzsche's warning: that the late Victorian Englishmen for whom 'morality is not yet a problem' would give way to a post-Victorian generation for whom morality would not only be problematic but nonexistent."[20] This was the case "because it tried to maintain itself without the sanctions and consolations of religion, but that was too impoverished, too far removed from its original inspiration, to transmit itself to the next generation."[21]

This specimen is especially interesting since it exemplifies the point made by a disciple of Thomas Aquinas, Jacques Maritain. Though the latter agreed with Newman that we cannot expect an inculcation of morality in education, yet he held that in any age of immorality more direct steps must be taken to enable the young to pursue virtue. On the other hand, where people are not religious and yet are virtuous, this is due to the vestiges of religion. The culture is Judaeo-Christian and even though, as in the instance of the Bloomsbury group, they do not practice religion, they nonetheless are supported in their striving for morality by these former structures.

While the move was taking place from Clapham to Bloomsbury, Soren Kierkegaard, an existentialistic thinker, and Newman both recognized the need for going beyond aesthetics and ethics to religion. If the culture did not recognize the need and follow its direction, then the road Newman considered incessantly would be traveled away from God and towards the self.

Frank Schaeffer on pages 8 and 9 in **Commentary** (February 1985) depicts the path:

> The great battle of the late 20th Century in America is not going to be between Christianity and Judaism, but rather between a commitment to religious principle and morality versus a rampant secularism that will, at first, seem to promote a pluralistic society in which Jews can breathe more freely, but that will finally destroy the essence of the concept of human rights. Thus, in a few short generations, the door will be opened to the type of value-free society in which all minorities, Jews included, will be threatened if they seem to stand in the way of the projects for human 'improvement' by the secular 'coercive utopians.'

This test case is clearly not conclusive, but it indicates that the issue of the **Apologia** and the **Grammar** is also the issue of the **Idea**. Annan captured the move towards pluralism by beginning his **Intellectual History** with the contrast between the limited options of Newman's time and the multiple options of Stephen's. His concerns were not those of Himmelfarb, but much has happened since 1979 and 1951. Lonergan could agree we have both an **a posteriori** and an **a priori** in Newman's position on the place of theology in the university.

APOLOGIA - INTEGRITY OF MIND

On page 100, Newman showed he was following the usual rules for a libel trial - he had to prove his state of mind even at the cost of a long digression on the Roman controversy. At first one would be hard pressed to show a connection between this and his life and opinions in 1839 so he felt it necessary to stress that the Oxford Movement was not only a negative force against Liberalism, but a positive force. Thus he had sought a positive theory. In the development of this theory, he came upon the Roman controversy.

His state of mind was neither that of doubt nor of expectation of doubt. "It was in this state of mind that I began to read up Bellarmine on the one hand, and numberless Anglican writers on the other." Here he showed that he could not advance his state of mind because he could find a disclaimer of "'Protestantism' but none for what he called 'Popery.'" Whereas Anglicans fell back upon the principle of Antiquity, Roman Catholics fell back upon that of Catholicity: "Apostolicity **versus** Catholicity."[1]

He then continued to narrate the "status of the controversy, as it presented itself to my mind." He did this by a series of extracts from his writings. These were misinterpreted by friends, as imprudent because they presented the case for Rome "with considerable perspicuity and focus," by his enemies as a betrayal. Whether friend or foe were correct, Newman had his own reasons: he was obsessed with examining the whole of an issue, with being fair to opponents and a duty to reveal the strength of Rome to his indolent Anglican associates. Lastly, friends who were tending towards Rome would not have been convinced to remain were he not to present Rome as well as the opposition could.

In summary, he noted that by 1835 and the start of 1836 he "Had the whole state of the question before him, on which to (his) mind, the decision between the churches depended."[2] Rather than the papacy, "the Faith and the Church was the issue of the controversy from beginning to the end. Thus the process of working out the differences between the claims of these two religions was "the history of (his) conversion."[3]

By 1840, Newman put the Anglican Church and himself to an **"experimentum crucis."**

> 'Our Church teaches the Primitive Ancient faith. I did not conceal this: in Tract 90, it is put forward as the first principle of all.' It is a duty which we owe both the Catholic Church, and to our own, to take our reformed confessions in the most Catholic sense they will admit: we have no duties towards their framers.
>
> I have thus put together, as well as I can, what has to be said about my general state of mind from the autumn of 1839 to the summer of 1841: and, having done so, I go on to narrate how my new misgivings affected my conduct, and my relations towards the Anglican Church.[4]

His method of thought was to reveal his way of facing difficulties. His first doubt about Anglicanism pertained to the note of Antiquity. He would face this doubt straight on; he would be an honest inquirer. Though only one person knew of his doubt, he would not conceal the principle he held was fundamental to justify his continuation in the Anglican Church: "'Our Church teaches the Primitive Ancient faith.'" Even if it could not show a universality comparable to the Catholic Church, it could show its Antiquity. If it were able to do so it would be by way of a sameness of doctrine. The 39 Articles would have to be interpreted in accord with "the belief of the Catholic Church as such. . . . In like manner I would say that the Articles are received, not in the sense of their framers, but . . . in the one Catholic sense.'"

By a parallel case, then, as the child is baptized on the faith of the Church, so the belief of the Catholic Church as such is to be the basis upon which to judge the sameness of doctrine.

His approach to doubt is clear: consider one's state of mind, how did this come about? Determine the principles in light of the issue. Follow a method of thought which accords with one or more parallel cases. The strength of the argument does not depend upon what is the best set of proofs, but what can be offered to an audience which has a state of mind open to it. This state of mind is open to the principle also. In this instance, Newman sought the most universal and uncontested principle he could find. Rather than to argue from a historical interpretation which would be open to controversy, he sought the most universal basis for holding the principle: the faith of the Church. If he were to succeed, then both the Anglican and the Catholic Church were the same in doctrine. Hence he called this an **experimentum crucis**. If he were to fail, then one or other Church would be false. In the latter case, he would be honest and give up. In proving the actuality of the experiment, and in demonstrating that it was no mere "feeler," Newman "did not draw back, but gave up." Through an examination of this crucial specimen on the basis of states of mind, methods of thought, and principle we are able to realize the true significance of Tract XC in Newman's relations with the Anglican Church.

Integrity Shown in His Style

In **English Prose** Arthur Galton reviews 500 years of writing and justifies this book of selections by claiming

> One of the great uses of a book of selection is to remind us that, in all ages, the really great writers have differed very little from one another; all good prose has the same qualities of directness, plainness, and simplicity. And good prose can still be written

whenever a writer condescends to think clearly, to stick
to the point, and to express his ideas in the plainest,
the simplest, and most direct and unpretentious way.[5]

Houghton concludes the **Victorian Frame of Mind**'s introductory chapter

with the two most outstanding features of the state of mind of the Victorian

society: "a bourgeois industrial state and widespread doubt about the nature

of man, society, and the universe."[6] With these there was also the impact

of the Puritan or Evangelical revival.

At the end of the work itself, Houghton makes the point which enables

a present day reader to understand both why Kingsley made the charge he

did and why Newman made so much of the charge. Nothing was "so often attacked

by the Victorians themselves as hypocrisy."[7]

A Letter to Pusey

Compromise Versus Integrity

Section 1 of the Introductory is an outstanding example of Newman's

concern with the state of mind of those who enter into a situation of compro-

mise. Edward Pusey had written an Eirenicon, a peace offering, in 1864.

Eventually Newman felt called upon to reply to it since his name was included

in it.

From earliest Oxford days, Pusey and Newman had been devoted friends,

until Newman left the Oxford Movement, sometimes called the Puseyite group,

and became a Roman Catholic. Thus Newman introduces his response in the

form of a letter to a friend. Most personally, he tries to put himself

in Pusey's state of mind. In the days of the Oxford movement, they had

taken strong criticism together. Now Pusey sees a time for bringing the

Anglican, Greek Orthodox, and Roman Catholic branches together. Newman

is hopeful from this sign from such an outstanding leader, but he does not

agree that the three are branches, nonetheless he knows the state of mind

Pusey has. Newman had been there.

In his search, he had followed "a faulty conscience, faithfully obeyed, through God's mercy, had in the long run brought me right." For this basic reason, he could claim "Fully, then, do I recognize the rights of conscience in this matter."

However, he noted that Pusey was very harsh in setting conditions. Even then, Newman tried to put the best face on these, as preliminaries to discussion. Yet these are a cause of horror for Anglicans, and a cause for indignation for Catholics, "not the most favourable conditions of mind for a peace conference."

From this section, we can agree that ecumenism, for Newman, presupposed an equality of trust upon the part of those who would enter into discussion as well as a favorable state of mind. This principle was later stated in Vatican Council II's Decree on Ecumenism.

Newman was dismayed Edward Pusey would not accept the principle of his **Essay on the Development of Christian Doctrine.** This would have enabled him to have worked out the patterns of the chief doctrines as they were held through history in the different churches.

Instead Pusey was interested in using the principle from Newman's Tract XC as modified by Cardinal Wiseman. Tract XC had interpreted the Council of Trent in such a way that an Anglican could simultaneously hold the 39 Articles and the teachings of Trent. Newman preferred the former principle, but he had concluded the introductory chapter by setting up the principle of holding what the Fathers of the Church had held. Since a response was already out to Pusey's stand on infallibility, Newman could hold to a critique of Pusey's stand on the Blessed Virgin Mary and not concern himself with infallibility. This stand of the Fathers was known as the teaching concerning

Mary as the New Eve. Since I have treated of this teaching at length elsewhere, this treatment of Newman's concern with principle in **A Letter to
Pusey** must suffice before we go on to a further treatment of states of mind
in the **Idea** as it relates to this issue of conscience.

States of Mind and Conscience

What was Newman's estimation of Julian the Apostate's state of mind
and how did he use this in his method of thought? At the heart of Discourse
VIII - "Knowledge Viewed in Relation to Religion" - Newman contrasted the
proud and amiable specimens of those who lead a spurious religion. Now
he highlights the characteristics of a spurious religion which is most difficult to discern because those who equate behavior and religion assume if
a person acts as we would wish, he or she is a truly religious person.
Only if we get into the person's state of mind, as **Callista** showed us, can
we determine whether a person is religious or not. Or, as we found in the
Apologia, only from states of mind can we determine how a person would act
if he or she were to be consistent.

Test Case: For Apologia

Why is it necessary to go beyond Walter Houghton's **The Art of the
Apologia?**

A careful analysis of Charles Harrold's review and Houghton's thesis
revealed their differences concerning the purpose of the **Apologia,** differences
which occurred because Harrold in his review ignored a crucial idea in
Houghton's argument. Though Harrold deeply appreciated the work and
recognized the similarity of Houghton's approach in prose to those of Cleanth
Brooks in poetry, yet he did not highlight the true significance of Houghton
or Newman because he bypassed the fundamental issue. Thus the insight of

the editor of the **Modern Language Notes** proved itself true despite the warning implied in his note to Harrold. He had warned that reviewers miss the author's point.

The comparison between Harrold's review copy and the review revealed a pattern in Harrold's manner of operation. In general, whatever was underlined, annotated, and cross-referenced in the review copy was proportionately found in the review and whatever was in the review could be found (thus marked) in the review copy. The major exception to this was the eighth chapter, "The Motive of Apology and Its Influence on Style" which was heavily underlined, annotated, and cross-referenced but was referred to in the review only by its title.

The other interesting omission was that of the Introduction. Not only did this not appear in the review, but it was not underlined, annotated, or cross-referenced; nevertheless it gave the basis for the structure of the work: Part I dealt with the **Apologia** from the standpoint of autobiography, Part II from that of apology, and Part III from the united focus of apologetic autobiography. All three were concerned with criticism. The introduction announced that the work was devoted to criticism from the perspective of art. Earlier Newman scholars had left this crucial approach "unexplored because criticism of prose, lagging as it does far behind that of poetry, has been content with general praise for Newman's power of self-analysis."[8]

In order to rectify this lack, Houghton had examined in the first part the theory of autobiography as developed by Newman, demonstrating that a study of the equipment which Newman brought to his task opened up "a series of perspectives from which to see the **Apologia**, and, by doing so, they widen our perceptions."[9]

In the second part, after having analyzed the method of the **Apologia** and its style, he had stressed the impact of the apologetic purpose upon the style.

In the third part, Houghton had used the apologetic autobiographical approach as a basis for evaluating the work as a whole. This Introduction and an examination of the eighth chapter demonstrated that Harrold's omissions had distorted the theory of criticism which Houghton had developed through his form analysis. Instead of depicting a fused pair of purposes, the review presented the autobiographical purpose as the dominant and the apologetic purpose as a mere chapter heading. Since the limits placed upon the autobiographical purpose by the apologetic purpose were extreme, the evaluation of Newman and the **Apologia** as autobiography would be distorted. Newman would seem to protest his honesty too much.

However, in moving from the review copy and the review to Harrold's own book, one finds an explanation for the two omissions. Harrold had a chapter "Autobiography" but he had nothing on an apologetic purpose. Nor did he allude to the listing of himself as one of the authors with whom Houghton disagreed concerning the purpose of the **Apologia**. The significance of this issue stood out because it introduced the chapter. Moreover in the review copy, Harrold underlined and cross-referenced this disagreement.

This disagreement was an important issue. Houghton had compared the autobiographical material in the **Apologia** with the like material in Newman's **Autobiographical Memoir** and indicated how the apologetic purpose changed the handling of this material.[10] But beyond this example of analysis was the more vital appreciation Harrold had in his review copy which he excluded from his review: "H. doing what never seems to have occurred to N. scholars-- going back to N's earlier writings and ideas to explain **Ap.**, OUS, GA, etc."[11]

In fact depending upon how one would count the parts and the whole works, Houghton used between 14 and 17 of Newman's writings and some 89 sets of pages from these writings. Again, that Harrold had not made a point of this comparative tool which is at the center of Houghton's method of analysis reminded one of the challenge placed by the editor.

Equally noteworthy was the omission of the thread of "states of mind" which Houghton traced throughout the **Apologia**. Houghton contrasted the different reasons for Newman's building up his states of mind against his "methods of thought."[12] Though Newman realized that arguments and methods of thought were necessary for the sake of the reader, he went out of his way to prepare the reader for each argument involved in the crises of his revolution of mind by a detailed description of his state of mind before and after each. Even where Newman confessed his inability to understand his motives or even his actions, as Houghton had seen,[13] he enabled the reader to side with him by providing the experience and his own state of mind as the experience had unfolded. Houghton illustrated his insight into the dramatic quality and the reason for the dramatic quality through this process of distinguishing states of mind from methods of thought.

Again, Harrold's omission of the "states of mind" point returns one to the fundamental disagreement, since this distinction and this emphasis upon states of mind provided the key to the apologetic purpose of the writing. Though the states of mind could have been used for both the purposes, nonetheless Houghton treated them in such a way that Harrold would have been hard pressed to cover them without entering into the disagreement directly. Although Harrold could not accept Houghton's reading of the purposes, he was able to agree on one of the subjects Houghton claimed for the **Apologia**: the work is about Newman's "anxieties and deliverances."[14] Though Harrold did not take space to summarize the reasons Houghton gave for Newman's exceptional readiness to recall these, the reasons are helpful in understanding the **Apologia**: Newman's acceptance of the reality of a personal Providence intervening in the minute stages of his life and his deep attachment to Oxford, resulted in his habit of reflecting upon the past.[15] Another subject Houghton highlighted but which Harrold passed over was that the **Apologia** described the "revolution of his mind."[16] In arguing for an apologetic purpose, Houghton noted that this passage was basic and an indication of the significance of this purpose in Newman's selection of material for his work.[17]

Regardless of these fundamental omissions, Harrold pushed us forward in our appreciation of Houghton by testifying in his review that "the author applies to Newman's prose the kind of minute but highly imaginative exploration which Mr. Cleanth Brooks so effectively applies to poems."[18] The section in which he had likewise marked his review copy was entitled, "Metaphor and Imagery." In chapter seven, "Style and the Dramatic Recreation of the Past," Houghton had indirectly criticized Harrold through his assertion that "the usual approach to Newman's style (was) so sterile and capping this by specifying what this was 'at its worst,'"[19] namely, the classification of Newman's styles into various categories. Harrold annotated this criticism in his review copy, indicating his own **Newman Treasury**. Harrold tried to put a better light on this in the review by arguing that "the fact remains, however, as even the author seems to admit on page 69, that Newman had no one style."[20] At that point, Houghton had depended upon Anne Mozley who "noted the subtle variation of his style, even in his letters, to harmonize with the known character of each correspondent."[21]

Rather than having listed or categorized styles, however, Mozley and Houghton seemed to agree that there were variations on a single style. Here Harrold seemed to have missed the fundamental advance Houghton had made over other Victorian critics in understanding Newman's style. Houghton was concerned to separate himself from the usual critic by a chapter long argument on Newman's "organic style."[22] Though Harrold had underlined Houghton's definition of organic style and bracketed it and annotated it with the comment that this was a summary, he omitted mention of it from his review. Since this topic is of paramount importance it will be of advantage to elaborate on this point.

Where Houghton had quoted a long section of the beginning of Part V (now edited as Chapter 3 of the **Apologia**) as the basis for his analysis of "four principal techniques" in the "re-creation of psychological life"[23] through Newman's organic style, he seemingly missed the recurrence of this passage in the next three techniques since he annotated as follows: "No more light here than that of Tardivel or Harrold. (too brief)." On page 49, the passage was quoted; on page 50, Houghton had analyzed it as an example of what he had earlier named "back-to-back" and completed this analysis with a second example. At this, Harrold claimed, "but only one example - the 'wavering' dilemma, etc."[24] In his review, Harrold wrote, "Part II is devoted to 'Method and Style'" - Newman's analytical method in action; to a close and highly illuminating study of his style, including syntax, metaphor, imagery, diction, rhythm, dramatic structure; and the 'motive of Apology and its influence on (his) style.'" ". . . I know of no more absorbing discussion of the mechanics and dynamics of literary style in action than Mr. Houghton's pages on Newman's syntax."[25]

Thus Harrold grasped the extraordinary feat though he faulted Houghton in his final paragraph of evaluation, and excused him on the grounds of brevity, for giving no "more than one illustration of how Newman's syntax reflects his mind." And even in this oversight, Harrold helped the future study of Victorian prose by reminding us that there are "other aspects of his mind manifested in the **Apologia** and these are not discussed."

However, he could have informed the reader that Houghton's footnotes contained listings of parallel occurrences which space did not allow him to expand. On the other hand, Houghton had actually given two examples of syntax: one a "back-to-back" and the second "back-and-forth." On page 29, Houghton had defined these and promised that he would give examples of them under the section on style. In working these examples out as well as in working out the examples for metaphor and imagery and dramatic structure, Houghton had kept the organic style of Newman in mind.

Because an understanding of Newman's organic style is, as was mentioned above, of paramount importance for those who would want to develop Houghton's critical methods further, it will be necessary to take a long quotation which he used throughout the seventh chapter and point out how he used this passage in each case. Though he used it in discussing each separate technique, he especially wanted to make it clear that the critical feature of Newman's style was the fact that it was a whole. Thus the reader must review the various instances and apply them to the whole passage.

Houghton assisted in this analysis beginning with an example which would fit under the dramatic structure technique, and which was listed as the fourth technique, before he entered into an analysis of the individual techniques:

> . . . and now that I am about to trace, as far as I
> can, the course of that great revolution of mind, which

led me to leave my own home, to which I was bound by so many strong and tender ties, I feel overcome with the difficulty of satisfying myself in my account of it, and have recoiled from doing so, til the near approach of the day, on which these lines must be given to the world, forces me to set about the task. For who can know himself, and the multitude of subtle influences which act upon him and who can recollect, at the distance of twenty-five years, all that he once knew about his thoughts and his deeds, and that, during a portion of life, when even at the time of his observation, whether of himself or of the external world, was less than before or after, by the very reason of the perplexity and dismay which weighed upon him, - when, though it would be most unthankful to seem to imply that he had not all - sufficient light, amid his darkness yet a darkness it emphatically was? And who can suddenly gird himself to a new and anxious undertaking, which he might be able indeed to perform well, had he full and calm leisure allowed him to look through everything that he has written, whether in published works or private letters? But, on the other hand, as to that calm contemplation of the past, in itself so desirable, who can afford to be leisurely and deliberate, while he practices on himself a cruel operation, the ripping up of old griefs, and the venturing again upon the 'infandum dolorem' of years, in which the stars of this lower heaven were one by one going out?[26]

Just before this passage, Houghton mentioned that this would reveal Newman's state of mind and "his normal modes of expression"[27] in his organic style: he would begin with a state of mind which would color the entire passage; he would give a dramatic tension in the presentation so that the reader would feel how great a problem Newman hoped to solve in writing of his "great revolution of mind;"[28] next, under the technique of syntax, Houghton provided a detailed example which showed how the example of "back-to-back" had been fulfilled in this passage; then he reminded us under the techniques of imagery and metaphor, of the "paragraph from which he started"[29] and "the muscular tension is immediately felt as Newman recoils"[30] from his task of tracing a revolution which led him to leave his very home, to which he was bound by "so many strong and tender ties,"[31] until the deadline "forces" to set about it. Houghton continued this analysis for a page in which he explained why the "infandum dolorem" was not pedantry but exactly the sort of experience we could well imagine Aeneas had in recounting the fall of Troy. Then to conclude with a juxtaposition of two forms of darkness: that of perplexity and that of the starless heaven. Moreover, Houghton began the section on diction and rhythm by returning us once more to the opening paragraph. Here he sought to have us hear the style of conversation as Newman spoke to himself of the task he was performing.

This example of Newman's organic style combines the state of mind, the syntax, the metaphor and imagery, the diction and rhythm, and the dramatic structure in such a few lines that only repeated readings give the full impact; unfortunately, Harrold missed this, yet was moved to compare another passage with the poetic criticism of Cleanth Brooks:

> I became excited at the view thus opened upon me. . . . After awhile, I got calm, and at length the vivid impression upon my imagination faded away. . . . I had to determine its logical value, and its bearing upon my duty, meanwhile, so far as this was certain, - I had seen the shadow of a hand upon the wall. It was clear that I had a good deal to learn on the question of the Churches, and that perhaps some new light was coming upon me. He who has seen a ghost, cannot be as if he had never seen it. The heavens opened and closed again. The thought for the moment had been, 'The Church of Rome will be found right after all;' and then it had vanished. My old convictions remained as before.[32]

Here, Harrold noticed how Houghton, in the manner of Brooks, minutely examined each element. First, the movement from the impact upon the mind and then the imagination was to be noticed. As the change from "excited" to "calm" joined the first sentence to the second, it also indicated how what was a mere view became a real view, yet only for a time. The image of light emerged in the pair of terms: "vivid" and "faded." Next the shift was back to the mind, then to the imagination once more. The view could be seen as the hand. A parallel was developed in the mindful approach to the Churches and the imaginary ghost. With this, the heavens were shown to open and close as we were startled by the revealing light. Houghton observed that "those verbs, incidentally are closely linked with the previous 'opened' and 'faded.'"[33] "Finally, in the summary sentence, idea and image, which so far have been alternation, are brilliantly fused in 'vanished,' which at once carried the 'view' as idea . . . and the 'view' as concrete image."[34] In all of this we have only sketched the depth and detail which Houghton contains. Thus Harrold could justly begin his review: "Here is one of the finest analyses of Newman's methods as writer in all Newman literature."[35]

In this statement Harrold was just, however, he refused to raise the fundamental positions Houghton had clarified: the apologetical autobiographical purpose of the **Apologia** and the organic style of Newman's prose, regardless of his appreciation that the **Art** is a masterpiece of Newman scholarship. In order to go beyond Harrold it is necessary to follow up on a point in his review: Houghton developed a prose theory of prose criticism analogous to Brook's theory of poetry.

Prose Critical Theory from Acceptance of Challenge

Harrold proved the editor of the **Modern Language Notes** correct since he largely ignored the fundamental positions of Houghton: the apologetical autobiographical purpose of the **Apologia** and the organic style of Newman's prose, and yet Harrold recognized the **Art** as a masterpiece of Newman scholarship. In order to go beyond Harrold it is necessary to approach the vital question: can Houghton's writing be the basis for searching into Newman for a theory of prose criticism analogous to that long popular in poetry through the lead of Brooks. In brief, we will answer this question by finding that Houghton has provided, through the insights Newman developed in his writings, but did not synthesize, an excellent plan of analysis which contains the seeds of a theory within it. The first part of his monograph offered the source of the plan, the second part carried it out in regard to the **Apologia**, and the third part used it as an instrument of evaluation.

In the first part, he acknowledged that Newman had at hand for his defense "theories of rhetoric, conceptions of man and the psychology of faith, ideas about the art of style and the nature of methods of biography including his own."[36] At the core of this theory of psychology was an assumption that "man is **not** a reasoning animal; he is a seeing, feeling, contemplating, acting animal."[37] As for theories of biography and style, Houghton discovered that these came together for Newman. On the one hand, the sources of biography were the letters and descriptions which caught the person he or she was at the time, and the style was to be conversational. Not just any conversation, but conversation as it took place in the common room at Oriel. In his **Further Letters of Gerard Manley Hopkins**, C. C. Abbott has preserved one of Hopkins' letters which revealed Newman's position exactly: "'Newman,' he wrote to Patmore, 'does not follow the common tradition of writing. His tradition is that of the cultured, the most highly educated, conversation; it is the flower of the best Oxford life.'"[38] Houghton considered this an example of how students of Newman felt we can get to Newman's inner life: "through the medium of living speech."[39]

Houghton concluded his critique of the **Apologia** by recalling T. S. Eliot's position on "the artistic handling of character: 'What the creator of character needs is not so much knowledge of motives as keen sensibility; the dramatist need not understand people; but he must be exceptionally aware of them."[40] This conclusion enabled him to exonerate Newman from the charge that in his apologetic autobiography he did not reveal the hidden well-springs of the evolution of his mind from his earliest days to his conversion. But the conclusion provided an explanation of Newman's organic style. We recall that just before presenting the techniques: syntax, metaphor and imagery, diction and rhythm, and dramatic structure, Houghton had defined Newman's style as organic and equated this with a "dramatic style."[41] Next he selected the crucial passage which would show that the four techniques coalesce in the single organic style and described this passage from Part V as a paragraph about the very person who was thinking and feeling the problem so that "the full sensibility (was) given dramatic expression."[42] Yet Houghton recognized that all of these examples of drama were preparatory to that which occurred on his leaving Oxford. By the use of two letters, Newman had made it obvious how great a sacrifice was involved. "You may think how lonely I am. **Obliviscere populum tuum et domum patris tui,** 'has been in my ears for the last twelve hours.'"[43] Therefore, Houghton concluded: "It is because we know his grief that the final passage carried dramatic pathos to the highest level."[44] "On the morning of the 23rd, I left the Observatory. I have never seen Oxford since, excepting its spires, as they are seen from the railway."[45]

Beyond centering the evaluation of the art of the **Apologia** on Newman's use of drama, Houghton found the technique of analysis Newman used provided well in advance in "Explicit and Implicit Reason" in the University Sermons. The earlier described distinction between states of mind and methods of thought were listed there: "'to designate particular methods of thought, according to which the mind reasons, (that is, proceeds from truth to truth) or to designate particular states of mind which influence its reasonings. Such method are antecedent probability, analogy, parallel cases, testimony, and circumstantial evidences; and such states of mind are prejudice, deference

to authority, party spirit, attachment to such and such principles, and
the like.'"[46]

Real Subject of Apologia

Yet Houghton warned that to ascertain Newman's states of mind and the
rest demanded exquisite patience, since one may have to read an entire work
to become aware of it, and even then, Newman may not be sure that it is
as it seemed to be. Although one is not sure at the end any more than Newman
was, one is able to grasp much more of what Newman is by how he is able
to pursue the truth. And this is the real subject of the **Apologia**: "His
subject was the evolution of his beliefs, he would have to show successive
states of mind both before and after each new doctrine was met and assimi-
lated."[47] As a romantic, Newman was willing to hold and savour an experience and then share it whether its meaning were evident or not since the
very experience and its impact led Newman to find something of value in
it regardless of anything beyond it. Houghton, probably with the help of
F. Cross, who refers to the same, found in "Tracts for the Times: No. 73
in Essays" an excellent citation of such a mentality: "Newman pled for the
value of half views and partial knowledge, of guesses, surmises, hopes and
fears, of truths faintly apprehended and not understood."[48] From all of
this, Houghton concluded that "Newman's analytic method in action gives
more attention to 'states of mind' than to 'methods of thought'"[49] and thus
he prepared the reader for his most helpful section on method and style.
But enough of this has already been given.

Houghton's Failure

Houghton wrote to thank Harrold for "the fine notice" which had appeared
in the March 1947 **Modern Language Notes**. Nonetheless it is obvious that

an analyst such as Houghton knew more about the limitations of the review than we do, granted that he did not have the annotated copy we possess; nor did he have the letter from the **Modern Language Notes** editor to warn him that the fundamental issues would be ignored; nor did he have a copy of **John Henry Newman** which Harrold was finishing as he wrote. On the other hand, he knew there was a difference of opinion over the purposes of the **Apologia** and he probably was satisfied that Harrold had read the eighth chapter despite its absence in the review. He may have held that Harrold did not have space in which to describe the organic style. On the other hand, the praise from the very leader of the field could have been a temptation to civility rather than to correction. It is more difficult to defend Harrold. His omissions are clear. His own stand is blatant. The road from the organic style to the apologetical autobiographical purpose is evident. Materially, Harrold's selections appear to have avoided the fundamental difference between him and Houghton. In doing his, he sheltered his position from an attack. An attack coming from Houghton or from those who understood Houghton, an author of what Harrold himself claimed was "one of the finest analyses of Newman's methods as a writer in all Newman literature."[50] As it was, the readers of the review would not have known this fundamental disagreement.

Conclusion

A collusion between an editor of such a reputable journal as **Modern Language Notes**, the leading authority on John Henry Newman, and the leading Victorian scholar seemed as improbable as the Watergate coverup, yet the evidence points to a serious breach of integrity on the part of each. The editor admitted that he expected little of book reviews. The Newman scholar recognized that the fundamental issue in criticizing the **Apologia** was the purpose. Nonetheless he avoided the very heart of the book under review which would have forced a confrontation between the position he took and the position of the book. Moreover, he ignored the excellent treatment of organic style Houghton discovered; the chief discovery in **The Art of the Apologia**: to have handled this treatment would have led him to contrast the purposes of the **Apologia**. On the other hand, Houghton accepted the review of his work as a "fine review."

The editor could have done what the present paper did. If he had, readers of the **Modern Language Notes** would have had an opportunity to appreciate the significance of Houghton's monumental discovery. Houghton himself could have complained of the deleterious omissions. Harrold would have had to examine his reasons for the omissions. Instead, the fields of book reviewing, of Victorian scholarship, and of the study of Newman have suffered.

Footnote:

This chapter, in large part, appeared originally as "An Academic Coverup in Autobiography and Its Reviewing: Newman's Challenge" in Volume 2 Number 1 Spring 1983, **Vitae Scholasticae.**

CALLISTA

I. States of Mind

Just as **The Idea of a University** is a source of a number of principles
in Newman's writings, so **Callista** is a source of a number of examples of
Newman's use of states of mind to prepare for his methods of thought. The
chief method of thought in this novel is the parallel case. Throughout
the novel, Newman is contrasting the states of mind of the pagan and the
Christian. Once we become aware of this approach we both feel the power
of the novel and situate the style of writing across genres in Newman.
Later we will find that the same use of states of mind gives a unity to
the **Apologia** as it does in this instance. And in similar fashion, the states
of mind prepare us for the methods of thought Newman employs.

In order to gain the most from the following analysis of **Callista** it
is necessary to take the symbol from Newman's **An Essay in Aid of a Grammar
of Assent** - the direction of movement a person can make from the same point.
One can either go towards or away from God. This symbol enters into both
the pagan experience and the Christian experience. Where the pagan takes
the direction towards God it is only a matter of time before he or she becomes
Christian; where the pagan takes the direction away from God it is only
a matter of time before there is no hope that the person will become a
Christian; instead, the person will have made the decision to remain a pagan
either implicitly or explicitly. This set of oppositions dramatized in
Callista is clear philosophically and theologically in the **Grammar**. Hence
in the references to the **Grammar** only an allusion will be made since later
there will be a detailed treatment in the chapter on the **Grammar**.

While this hopeful and simplified symbol worked as it did for Newman,
here writing from a Catholic viewpoint, it also worked for Leslie Stephen,

the noted agnostic and critic of Newman, who accepted and used Newman's approach and methods of thought in an opposite fashion in his own synthesis, **An Agnostics' Apology** which combined the **Grammar** and the **Apologia** for critical and for personal reasons. He had taken the issues raised by the symbol and gone in the opposite direction. Thus the thought Newman exerted apologetically, resulted in assisting his opponents as well as himself. Hence, though, as Newman stated in his preface, the work is written for the edification of Catholics, the result is of value regardless of one's position.

This symbol of ascent and descent which Newman described at length in Note 2 of the **Grammar** appears in Callista's crisis. She ascends from heathenism to Catholicity gradually, step by step. As she does, she interacts with the others. They experience their own strengths and weaknesses through her. She is at times conscious of her state of mind and at others she pulls back from her deep consciousness unable to live in complete awareness. In the intricate combination of these ways she lived what Bernanos' future **Joy**, whose goodness is such that she destroys the lukewarm characters in her surroundings, would live.

The psychological aspects later examined in the **Grammar** served in **Callista** as a mask for the spiritual battles Newman sketched. To gain an insight into these we begin with the clear exposition of the states of mind in **Callista**. The novel opens with a contrast between the states of mind of the pagans and the Christians. Already in the second chapter, the issue of the ascent and the descent is powerfully marked. Juba, the brother of Agellius, Callista's unrequited lover, shows himself a demon, but more significantly, as stuck in the door of the Church. Whereas others will go forward or away, Juba remains caught.

The "New Generation" chapter opened with an expression of the traditional principles according to which Jucundus lived. How he lived these principles was beside the point. The principles enlightened the meaning of his state of mind. This was enough. Jucundus learned that Arnobius, a young teacher of rhetoric, was on to a correct principle: an agnostic-atheistic principle, because he could find no better than what was now taught even though neither the teachers nor the learners believed in it. "No, better stay where I am" of Arnobius resulted in "That's the true principle" of Jucundus. With this Arnobius carried out his duty to Rome without belief, thus avoiding conflict with Agellius. Arnobius was confident that Christianity was on the way out, and especially in fickle Agellius' state of mind; that of a stubborn, yet fickle believer.

Italo Calvino's **Manzoni's 'The Betrothed:' The Novel of Ratios of Power** not only gives us the significance of the need to unite thought and language, so crucial to Newman's **Idea,** but also to the relation of principle and states of mind. Manzoni does this by considering the plight of the illiterate and the state of mind of the intellectual. In a long paragraph which, in a way, constitutes the finest in the whole book, he compares the letter which the peasant needs written and the process of the interaction between the simple peasant and the literate with his skill in the use of words. Jucundus typifies the wise, manipulative latter, while Arnobius typifies the naive peasant. When the peasant tells what he wants on paper, the literate writer takes over the control and puts on paper what he wants. In fact, he puts on paper something entirely different from what he had been asked. Manzoni, long experienced with publishers, notes how often this very thing has happened to him where the **printed word** was far from what he had sent into the publisher. The situation becomes clearer to us as we note what happens to the peasant's letter now. When the second peasant to whom the letter had been written receives it he must go to another literate person both to learn what the letter says and to reply.

This intricacy is what makes this such an excellent example of the value of a principle - states of mind - method of thought approach. Not only do we have the translation by Patrick Creagh's translation of Calvino's edition of Manzoni, but also Archibald Colquhoun's translation of Manzoni. A close reading of the two shows how apt Manzoni's point is. The first major difference in translation comes at this point about the publisher. Colquhoun put it thus: "It even happens to us who write for the Press." Shortly after we read: "Questions arise as to how it is to be understood; for the interested party, basing himself on his knowledge of past facts, asserts that certain words mean one thing; while the reader, basing himself on his experience in composition, asserts that they mean another." Finally the most significant difference comes in the conclusion: "then, however brief the correspondence, the two parties end by understanding each other about as well as two scholars did in the older days after arguing for four hours about abstract mutation not to take a simile from live issues, in case we stir up a hornet's nest."[2]

Clearly the original and the two translations all prepare the reader for the next section of **The Betrothed**, yet we notice a distinct difference of the state of mind of the two translators. This state of mind is the issue for Newman. He knew that style should show a unity of thought and language and hence he knew how difficult translating could be, not only of Scripture, but of any Classic.

Herbert Read had come upon the limits of composition and rhetoric. He confessed that in order to understand the unity of Newman more was necessary - the reader had to understand his "predominating passion." Until this became known Newman's subtlety would be unexplainable. And this predominating passion was rooted in his faith; therefore readers such as Leslie Stephen would feel Newman's passion without understanding it. Instead Stephen wrote his reply or response to Newman as an agnostic. He could use the methods and the states of mind approach of Newman without accepting his principles.

This difference over principle somewhat clarifies the lack-lustre response **Callista** occasioned. Unless the reader took Stephen's approach to the novel, the value and the significance of the amazing treatment of states of mind and methods of thought could be wasted. On the other hand, in the next section of this chapter we will find the power of both the states of mind approach and the methods of thought approach regardless of the acceptance or rejection of Newman's principles.

II. Methods of Thought

In December 1880 as he was about to send a new edition of the **Grammar** to press, Newman revealed the ascending and descending scales of thought he had described dramatically in **Callista** and in a variety of ways in the **Apologia** and **Discourses to a Mixed Congregation** by answering the charge Fairbarn made in the public press: "Cardinal Newman has **confined** his defense of his own **creed** to the proposition that it **is the only possible** alternative to Atheism."[3]   In the first place, Newman brought out the implications of the charge: 1) there are no arguments from reason, either from religious conviction or from rhetorical skill, by which a defense of the Catholic faith could be made, and 2) that Fairbarn had merely used scare tactics by pretending to show the public that for Newman there is no choice except Catholicism if Atheism is to be rejected.

Then, Newman recalled that his position was available in the **Grammar**. Reviewing the many arguments, one would not find any evidence for the charge, because no where does the alternative appear: 1) they are wrong who hold that we cannot believe what we cannot understand; 2) causation and law reveal a Creator; 3) certitude can be achieved through a cumulation of proofs without need for demonstration; 4) next, a direct proof of theism from three departments of phenomena; 5) then to the proof of Christianity by the recall of prophecy, the testimony of the Old and New Testament, and the testimony of the primitive martyrs from Catholicism. In none of these instances did he speak of the alternative.

After listing four other controversial efforts in defense of his creed, where no mention of atheism occurred, Newman disclosed the **ex officio** passage on page 198 of the **Apologia** "'there is no medium, in true philosophy, between Atheism and Catholicity, and that a perfectly consistent mind, under those circumstances in which it finds itself here below must embrace either one or the other.'" As so often is the case, Newman answers this specific problem for Fairbarn and other readers by removing the threat from the issue. He does this by arguing through a parallel case in Butler, whose **Analogy of Religion** was always at hand, Butler could find no **medium** between the acceptance of the Gospel and the denial of a Moral Governor. Yet a reader of Butler would not feel threatened on the one hand, nor claim that he had no reasonable defense.

Nor, again, would a reader be justified in holding that Newman only depended upon Butler's analogy between nature and grace, since Newman was clear that Butler's argument was, as a whole, a negative argument and thus inadequate for convincing one of the truth of Christianity. Rather the analogy clears the past states of mind which had blocked the inquiry, but more is needed as Newman put in the **Discourses**:

> When once the mind is broken in, as it must be, to the belief of a Power above it, when once it understands that it is not itself the measure of all things in heaven and earth, it will have little difficulty in going forward. **I do not say it will, or can go on to other truths without conviction; I do not say it ought to believe the Catholic Faith without friends and motives**; but I say that, when once it believes in God, the great obstacle to faith has been taken away, a proud, self-sufficient spirit, etc.[4]

A new state of mind will be open to argument! And with such, one can even grasp the positive nature of the analogy. Where we have the coincidental testimony of two witnesses, we have a positive argument to the existence of the event. Mediation is obvious in both the world and in Scripture. Newman extends the point by listing the meaning of testimony in the **Apologia**: 1) the objective matter of both Natural and Revealed Religion; 2) the character of the evidence, and 3) the legitimate position and exercise of the intellect towards the evidence. By examining the evidence for Mediation in these three meanings, he was on the way to the discovery of an **organum investigandi**. At first he resolved his inquiry into "The Variations of Papacy," then in a law of development, and next, in the need for a Presence if the development were to be explained. From this movement within his own perception, he came to the application to the Evidences of Religion and statement on Atheism and Catholicity.

An analysis of this process and the need for a process by which different questions are faced and resolved led him to search for an **organum investigandi** for religious truth and which would follow an ascending order from atheism to theism, from theism to Christianity to Evangelical Religion, and from there to Catholicity. This ascending order and descending order are examined in the **Grammar**. And Newman reveals that a main reason for writing the **Apologia** and in **Callista**, but the fact that there is a descending as well as an ascending scale left Fairbarn open to misinterpreting the statement. Fairbarn considered only the descending as a threat. "If you are not Catholic, you must be an Atheist, and will go to Hell." Newman considered both and stressed the ascending which **Callista** experiences, thus "I am a Catholic, for the reason that I am not an Atheist."

To defend his interpretation, Newman first quotes a passage written long before the **Apologia** in which he tells his Protestant friends to grasp one truth really and they will be on the ascending path and then on November 18, 1880, letter of Mr. Lilly who on the very day of the publication wrote a most competent defense in which he challenged Fairbarn: "I cannot venture to ask you to allow me space to do more than thus indicate the nature of the argument by which he ascends from his first to his final religious idea."[5]

The principle of an ascending and descending order in the movement of the illative sense is crucial to Newman's understanding of conversion. On pages 198-204 of the **Grammar** we have the instance of changing religions without changing principles. A Protestant, a Unitarian, and a Catholic are specimens of the change. The question to ask is: what did they originally really assent to and what now? There is a psychological thrill as we consider these specimens, yet we do not enter into them. Obviously we are considering them abstractly, objectively, and from a distance. However, we have the opportunity in **Callista** to become involved. But to return to the **Grammar**: Newman puts the question:

> When, then, we are told that a man has changed from one religion to another . . . have the first and second religions nothing in common? To answer this question, Newman reviews the relation between doctrines and beliefs. His three Protestants can move to Catholicism, Unitarianism, and unbelief without ever having left home because, 'each of these men started with just one certitude.'[6]

Each "was true to that one conviction from first to last." Each had merely added to their "initial ruling principle, but he has lost no conviction of which he was originally possessed."[7] This is the heart of conversion: our ruling principle. So that we will not miss this, Newman takes the example of a person converted to the Catholic Church who falls away. The reason for his falling away is the reason he should not have been received in the first place, "he never had the indispensable and elementary faith of a Catholic."[8] Any change in the doctrines of the Church can be an excuse for such a person to leave, because he did not hold the doctrines unconditionally, but conditionally. In this example, the person put the condition "those particular doctrines 'which at that time (of my conversion) the church in matter of fact formally taught.'"[9]

What Newman is considering are our three themes: principles, states
of mind, and methods of thought. We seem to change from what we were certain
of to any other stage of ascent or descent, but in reality, the point of
the scale is in accord with our state of mind and our principles so that
we argue with these as a foundation. After reviewing what heathens have
held which in principle is the same as what a Christian held, Newman moved
on to the various religions to conclude:

> And thus it is conceivable that a man might travel
> in his religious profession all the way from heathenism
> to Catholicity, through Mahometanism, Judaism, Unitarian-
> ism, Protestantism, and Anglicanism, without any one
> certitude lost, but with a continual accumulation of
> truths, which claimed from him and elicited in his intel-
> lect first and fresh certitudes.[10]

Though Newman presented the ascent most positively, nonetheless he
recognized its limitations and the objections others would raise. A principle
is expressed differently in the various religions. This is due to the formal
character of the whole of each religion. No principles exist in vacuums.
Rather the original growth and development comes from the principle and
when this occurs the accidentals surround both the principles and the truths
stressed through the perception. However, the individual believer who joins
this group may accept the principle in a way which is compatible with another
group's faith.

On the other hand, it can be objected that certitudes do "perish in
the change." When people move from religion to religion, they face radical
differences in principles and methods of thought which result in an entirely
new state of mind. Are certitudes, then defectible? Newman could have
taken the easy way out by claiming that what are certitudes, if the result
of errors, are not certitudes, or the manner in which someone held the certitudes was merely prejudice and not validly held; instead he took the two

test cases: 1) Jews who became Christians in the first days of Christianity and Jews who did not, 2) Anglicans who became Catholics and those who did not. His rebuttal consisted in dividing the Jews themselves on the basis of their certitude in relation to the law or to the principle of good will and openness towards salvation, with the latter joining the Christians, and in dividing Anglicans into those seeking a perfect way or those who reacted in their faith as a mean between extremes, with the former joining the Church.

Yet another large group are those prejudicial against the Church who are vulnerable as their prejudices are. Thus there are no arguments for the defectibility of certitude since "persistence in such prejudices is no evidence of their truth, so an abandonment of them is no evidence that certitude can fail."[11]

When Newman felt his task done on indefectibility of certitude, he went on to formal inference, where he first had to show the strengths and weaknesses of logic. After a long exposition, he questioned the value of logic with its many limitations: "the long introspection lodges us at length at what are called first principles, the recondite source of all knowledge, as to which logic provides no common measure of minds, . . . in which, and not in syllogistic exhibitions lies the whole problem of attaining to truth."[12] Here the greatest difficulties exist . . . how to find and secure our principles.

Because logic does not get to the source of knowledge, we must have something more than it, "we require an **organon** more delicate, versatile, and elastic than verbal argumentation."[13] Or, "as to Logic, its chain of conclusions hangs loose at both ends; both the point from which the proof should start, and the points at which it should arrive, are beyond its reach;

it comes short both of first principles and of concrete issues."[14]

Because formal inference, logic cannot get to the concrete, Newman developed a thorough treatment, of informal inference and of natural inference. Here Newman first concludes that just as it is clear that logic is inadequate; that there is a way to handle the concrete. The method is informal inference. The process is an accumulation of probabilities, on the one hand, and a series of independent arguments on the other. In the process, we first examine our state of mind and our grasp of the methods of study required. When we are secure, we carry out a study of the concrete matter directed towards a judgment. From this deliberation we go on to the conclusion and finally to the fact that we are certain of this conclusion. This process has been carried through "by a mental comprehension of the whole case, and a discernment of its upshot."[15]

Newman reviewed this process to contrast it with formal inference, which is the same but deals with abstractions, while informal inference deals with concrete data. The mind reasons as a whole, depending upon an implicit principle of discrimination, because it does not analyze its motives, but lets itself open to the entire evidence. The end of this process is yet conditional as is formal inference, but a factor added is that each person needs a different cumulation of probabilities "And this . . . without prejudice to the objective truth or falsehood of propositions."[16] In this description of how the mind operates when it is carrying out an informal inference is a description of Newman's experience in writing the **Apologia**.

That different minds need different motives and evidence was obvious to Newman, but a problem for his skeptical friends; therefore he prepared a number of illustrations, but first distinguished reasoning as "the exercise of a living faculty in the individual intellect, and mere skill in argumentative science."[17] In considering our human ways, Newman felt for the scientist and for the ordinary person. The scientist had to endure the implicit form of reasoning at the cost of his sense of outrage; while the ordinary person experienced a deepfelt prejudice against logic because it does not do what the ordinary person expects, and it acts so impudently.

Thus Newman summarized the prejudice against Logic: "its formulas make a pedant and a **doctrinaire**, that it never make converts, that it leads to rationalism, that Englishmen are too practical to be logical, that an ounce of common sense goes farther than many cartloads of logic, etc."[18] Newman continues concerning Hume and miracles that originally they were accepted "against their (the believer) method."

In the analogy of the Cave, Plato portrays the prisoner changing from an unenlightened to an enlightened person. From the state of mind which preferred the dark, and the shadows and echoes, to a state of mind which preferred reality, the light, and the truth. This change is global and specific. At first, the image is general enough for anyone; later we recall that the **Republic** shows us the social whole in order to show us the individual. We would not be able to notice the individual due to its size, but we can notice the state. So in the cave, we originally go up and down once, but the very curriculum and the divided line remind us that any number of returns must be made. Each new study originally puts us back in the cave until we have a sufficiently general enlightenment so we can start at a higher level, but even in the light of the sun we are blinded and must seek out the night, the shadows, and the reflections.

John Henry Newman modified this image somewhat but he continued to use the symbol of blindness. And even more significantly, he continued to grasp the importance of the state of mind Plato had in mind. This change and this awareness pervaded his writing on a pastoral, evangelical, and rhetorical level. As he wrote **Callista,** he compared and contrasted the states of mind of the many characters. What he portrayed in **Callista** he spelled out in the **Grammar of Assent.** As he wrote **Loss and Gain,** he compared and contrasted the states of mind of the many characters. What he portrayed in **Loss and Gain,** he narrated in the **Apologia.** What he had in these he preached in his **Oxford University Sermons.** Gradually he clarified his own state of mind and retained a memory of his earlier states. This complex change he gave us in the **Essay on Christian Development.** On the other hand, he showed the operation by which this change could be brought about in his **Idea of a University.**

Callista, then, begins with the notice that the pagan state of mind differs from the Christian state of mind. Already in Chapter 2 the sharp contrast between the devil and the Christian state of mind is delineated by the contrast between Juba and Agellius. Whereas Agellius is just within the church door, Juba is caught in the door of the church. This most unusual character will later show how abnormality can result from a conflict between the opportunity extended and its refusal.

In the next chapter we have the most significant allusion to states of mind in the novel: on page 78, "In this state of mind the old gentleman (Jucundus) determined one afternoon to leave his shop to the care of a slave, and to walk down to his nephew, to judge for himself of his state of mind."

Newman raised his issue early but held back from revealing the answer for some thirty pages in which he described Agellius' state of mind for us. Agellius had been attracted to Christianity and had begun, yet the attractiveness of Callista delayed Christ. Callista herself opened Agellius' eyes: "Is this the reason why you gave me flowers, Agellius, . . . for a funeral urn?"[19]   Her speech before Agellius brings about the start of his apocertersis.   In Aristotle we have the discovery and the reversal.   Oedipus searches from the prophet, from Creon and the Delphic oracle, from one shepherd after another when he can get beyond Jocasta's misleading interpretations, until the final shepherd clinches Oedipus' identity.   Oedipus had insisted the shepherd speak and he listen.   With this revelation, he understands and there is a reversal.   He need no longer search.   The symbols of the play reverse: the searcher, is the one found; the blind see.

Agellius sees himself as he is: an idol worshipper.   He must relinquish Callista and seek out Christ.   Jucundus had sized up his nephew's state of mind well.

Callista's State of Mind in the Period of Her Imprisonment

Newman understands that the crux of the matter is Callista's state of mind at the time of her death.   Therefore he enters into her mind during her imprisonment only to find at first that she is not conscious of her state of mind; she is not conscious of her consciousness.   She has not yet reflected upon where she stands in relation to Christianity.   Gradually Newman unveils the basis upon which she has started towards a new state of mind .   This basis is the crucial consideration in his thought: the place of witnesses, the place of independent witnesses to the Divine Presence.   On a wider stage, he would seek out a difference of African, Eastern and Western witnesses, but on this smaller scale, he recognizes Chioe, a slave and thus an uneducated person, then Agellius a Greek, and finally Cyprian, an African Father of the Church.   Each shapes Callista's state of mind in a different but common manner, they agree in grasping religion as a personal relationship. They know in their hearts. This knowledge has a content: she reflects upon the doctrines they have taught her but her faith is grounded in their witnesses and it is directed toward an Object. She has an informal inference.

Here we recall the fifth chapter of the **Grammar,** as well as the eighth. In the former, we find Newman admitting that he is not trying to prove God's existence, but that it is

> . . . impossible to avoid saying where (he will) look for the proof of it. For . . . that proof (is) in the same quarter as that from which (he) would commence a proof of His attributes and character, by the same means as those by which (he) shows how we apprehend Him, not merely as a notion, but as a reality.[20]

Thus he is moving to put Callista in a situation where we can watch her act upon her conscience. Aristotle attempts to support her in freeing herself from the charge of being a Christian, but she is more concerned to have a Christian priest come to her. Yet before she can receive his ministrations she is brought before the sedellia to prove she is not a Christian. As she takes up the incense, she realizes that it is against her conscience. She throws the incense down. Her informal inference has not yet brought her to conviction, but it has freed her from her false religions and prepared her for her conversion.

Over and over we find a harmony and consistency of Newman's principles and methods of thought. Certain issues raised by Locke and others cause him to rebut them from a variety of angles. So frequently he refers us to the **Grammar** as his longest and deepest treatment and to the **University Sermons** as a starting point. The very difficulty of the issues and the slowness of the change in his state of mind is brought forth in this inter- action of the many writings, and especially in his two novels where the characters only gradually move from apprehension to inference to assent.

The link between his change and his characters' change will be found in the following digression.

The **Essay of Development** is introduced by Newman's favorite method of thought: parallel cases. "The most natural hypotheses, the most agreeable to our mode of proceeding in parallel cases, and that which takes precedence over all others, is to consider that the society of Christians, which the Apostles left on earth, were of that religion to which the Apostles had converted them."[21] Thus he concludes his introduction

> . . . the following Essay is directed towards a solution not of the difficulty which has been stated. - The diffi-culty, as far as it exists, which lies in the way of our using in controversy the testimony of our most natural informant concerning the doctrine and worship of Christi-anity, viz. the history of eighteen hundred years . . . that from the nature of the human mind, time is necessary for the full comprehension and perfec-tion of greatest ideas; and that the highest truths, though communicated to the world once at roughly the period of catacomb Christianity. Happily there were intellectual and spiritual counterparts close enough to the nineteenth century to warrant this angle of approach. However, the main value of this historical period was that it was an age of conversion. Men of all classes came to assent to the Christian faith in lieu of immense profane distraction and mundane intellec-tuality.[22]

What was their path of assent? Walter Pater knew that religious commitment was intensely personal, and he was fully aware that the religious state arose from needs felt from the contact of real experience. So **Marius** is an autobiographical process which shows the development of the religious nature of man as he moves toward Christ in conversion. Briefly, Pater traces the journey of a young man from his simple pagan piety through various stages of hedonism and stoic correctives to Christian belief.

Carlyles' **Sartor Called Resartus** is sometimes compared to Newman's work, but it does not go as far as Pater's **Marius** - to religion. He knows there is something wrong with his time, but he hopes education will cure it. It doesn't. Newman does the same but succeeds and Pater follows him. Obviously, the issues of the Victorian period required some recovery.

Geoffrey Faber, whose grandfather was Rev. Francis Atkinson Faber, whose younger brother was Father Frederic Faber, tells us in a preface which justifies his critique of Lytton Strachey's essay on the Oxford movement that "the Tractarians were determined to have something, which we have accustomed ourselves to do without - certainty upon the terms and the purpose of their earthly apprenticeship."[23] He dedicated it to T. S. Eliot in 1933. On page 230 of the **Oxford University Sermons**, Newman corrects the Illative Sense and the educated:

> If children, if the poor, if the busy, can have true Faith, yet cannot weigh evidence, evidence is not the simple foundation on which Faith is built. If the great bulk of serious men live, not because they have examined evidence, but because they are disposed in the certain way, - because they are 'ordained to eternal life,' this must be God's order of things. . . . What, then is the safeguard, if Reason is not?[24]

"The safeguard of Faith is a right state of heart. . . . It is holiness, which is the quickening and illuminating principle of true faith, giving it yes, hands, and feet. It is Love which forms it out of the rude chaos into an image of Christ; or, in scholastic language, justifying faith . . . **fides formata charitate.**"[25]

For the next two pages, Newman enters into the spirit of the Good Shepherd. We are sought by God - our faith is not a question of our reasoning, but of God loving us and seeking us. Thus he corrects his term love in a footnote where he calls it **credendia pia affectio.** We will to believe. We have been sought by the Good Shepherd. We are sheep. To clinch this approach, Newman goes to St. Paul, "For who hath known the mind of the Lord, that he may instruct Him? But we have the mind of Christ."[26] Here a certain moral state, and not evidence, is made the means of gaining the Truth, and the beginning of spiritual perfection.

Footnote: George Klubertanz confirmed Newman's process:

> Demonstrative knowledge has two stages: first, the
> stage of discovery or inquiry; second, that of critical
> evaluation of judgment upon the conclusions reached;
> or in other words, a stage of induction and a second
> stage of organization and evaluation, **(via inventionis,
> via judicii)** . . . **"method of 'intelligible induction.'"**
> **. . . very complicated process of discovery we can call**
> **'rational induction.' 'Secondly, . . . many different**
> **methods, and sometimes quite distinctive ones . . . conse-**
> **quently, most of what is written about scientific method**
> **rest on confusion and on unwarranted assumptions.'**[27]

III. Principles

The New Generation chapter opened with the traditional principles upon
which Jucundus lived. How he lived these principles was beyond the point.
The principles enlightened the meaning of his state of mind.

In order to deepen our understanding of Agellius' state of mind, Newman
reviewed both his education and his conversations with Aristo and Callista.
At the Temple of Mercury, Agellius studied what those of his time ordinarily
did, yet it opened his mind to the Christian teachings; while his conversations with his two Greek friends as well as the experience of Greek tragedy
and comedy dramatized by Aristo and Callista raised the perennial questions
he would have to solve. But the conflict of pagan and Christian principles
did not arise.

The principles upon which Jucundus and Aristo based their lives were
opposed to conversion. Arnobius, an agnostic atheist, could discover neither
teachers nor learners who were committed to any other belief, so he concluded,
"No better stay where I am." Jucundus agreed "That's the true principle."
Through this agreement, Arnobius was in a position to carry out his duty
to Rome without a conflict with Agellius. In fact, Arnobius was confident
that Christianity was on the way out - especially in fickle Agellius' mind.

How did the latter give Arnobius such an impression of his state of mind: Agellius' religion was unknown to the majority of the citizens of Sicca; Jucundus would use this fact in arguing for a clandestine marriage of Callista and Agellius. No one would be surprised that he put incense in the Temple because they saw him as a normal loyal citizen. Any impact of Christian principles upon his state of mind and method of thought was hidden - both from himself and the world.

The unsettled condition of Agellius' state of mind convinced Jucundus that an equally unsettled Callista would be worth the risk in the conspiracy to shake Agellius' faith in order to insure he would not become a martyr.

Since we could only note the fact of Agellius' fickle state of mind from Arnobius' representation, it was imperative for Newman to find a proper way to describe Agellius' state of mind. This he did through a report on Aristo and Callista in frequent meetings at their shop, at which the conversation resembled a liberal education as would have been available in Greece at the time.

Only later by the good intercession of Cyprian would Agellius' brother be freed after a long period of going in the wrong direction and madness. At the same time, Agellius begins life as a mediocre Christian. At first the state of mind of Agellius, was of no concern to Jucundus, a pagan uncle. "In this state of mind the old gentleman determined one afternoon to leave his shop to care for a slave, and to walk down to his nephew, to judge himself of his state of mind."[28] On the way, Jucundus, comes upon Arnobius, a skeptic who denies the gods yet worships them. And he shows where he is "but where shall I go for anything better? Or why need I seek anything good or bad in that line? Nothing's known anywhere, and life would go while I attempted what is impossible. No, better stay where I am; I may go further, and gain a loss for my pains."[29] "That's the true principle," answered the delighted Jucundus."[30] Agellius began conversing with Aristo and Callista, "he had no suspicion at the time that those who conversed so winningly, and sustained so gracefully and happily the commerce of thought and sentiment, might in their actual state, may, in their governing principles, be in utter contrariety to himself."[31] Thus principles and states of mind were contrasted on page 112. Agellius has been compromised by Jucundus, who made arrangements with Aristo to have Agellius propose to Callista. At this point, Agellius sees Callista at the beginning of the move to Catholicism. "He had a perception, which he could not justify by argument, that there was in Callista a promise of something higher than anything she yet was." Then we have the death of Atheism on 116-117. "Indeed, without them, how should we have had means to come here. But there's a weariness in all things." Callista sings a song of death of the Sun god. Now, "but somehow I worship nothing now. I am weary."[32]

In the proposal discussion, Callista uses the flowers Agellius brings for love as a symbol of death. "Is this the reason why you give me flowers, Agellius, that I may rank with Chione?"[33] She is a Christian slave of Callista's who had a dream shortly before her death of an angel of death. "You are offering me flowers, it seems, not for a bridal wreath, but for a funeral urn."[34] He will tell her his state of mind. Agellius and Callista, as noted on page 112, were one. Now he wants to be able to convert her to Christ. She sees he is using his Master to win her. He had not led her to the Master. She sees he is cold, selfish, and narcissistic. He worshipped her rather than the Master. He spoke of himself. "She had supplied the true interpretation of his giving."[35] Callista sees that Jucundus and Aristo wanted her to "bring him low."[36] "It was a strange contrast, the complaint of nature unregenerate on the one hand, the self-reproach of nature regenerate relapsing on the other."[37] Agellius realized Callista is not for him, but for his Master. He will watch from a margin as she moves towards the Master. Jucundus was right about Agellius' state of mind.

Principle Conflict

Note 2 of **Grammar** refers to the statement in the **Apologia** that there is no stop other than atheism or Catholicism. This 1870 statement was worked out dramatically in **Callista**. The novel begins with a contrast of the state of mind of the pagan and the Christian. In the second chapter, Juba as a demon, is stuck in the door of the Church. Principles kept him from appreciating some Greek comedy. This loss of sensitivity by the Greeks was not apparent to Aristo; Agellius had developed this almost naturally.

On the other hand, his brother Juba and Jucundus were aware of Agellius' danger of a conflict of principle. Human respect was still strong in him; therefore Jucundus suggested a clandestine marriage between Callista and him. "Who knows you have been a Christian?" With no witness to Christianity from Agellius, Jucundus felt free to propose a marriage **consuetudine**: a marriage merely by custom with no public ritual, but only after listing forms of marriage which would have been ever more abhorrent to Agellius who had the hope that Callista would become a Christian and free him from a choice between them of the type of conjugal celebration to have.

Agellius, faced with an imminent marriage with a pagan, reacted against **matrimonium consuetudine** with sufficient horror to alert Jucundus to his mistake in entering into Agellius' state of mind. To rectify this, he compared such a marriage with a mere **con tubermium**, a concubinage and stressed how briefly the thought had remained in his mind. But Agellius made it clear that none of the heathen forms of marriage would suit him. Only Callista's conversion would make marriage possible and make an undowered Greek and a positioned Roman equal, however Agellius realized that he did not know Callista's state of mind. The conversations revealed a person who could tend to Christianity, not one who actually did so.

Now Jucundus prepared the way for his nephew to learn more of her state of mind by arranging with Aristo for Agellius' proposal. This caused a conflict between his understanding and his conscience. Much as he might make it seem Callista would change, in his conscience he knew it was his desire which colored his understanding. Hence he went to propose with trepidation. He entered into a heathen city from the openness of his country trembling, but unaware of the chasm separating Pagan Rome and Christian Africa. Unaware of the meaning of the work of Aristo and Callista, preparing images for the temples and shrines of the pagan religion, Agellius was also unaware that Aristo like Jucundus expected that Callista would be able to recover him from Christianity. Nor that Callista deprecated his Christianity if he were willing to marry her.

During the wait, Callista's state of mind is more delicately revealed. She is weary of the life of pursuit. Engagements have lost their appeal. Her very weariness discloses the Epicurean tastes of Aristo. Suddenly she sings her parting prayer to the sun god. No longer does this hold her devotion. In fact, considering Aristo's selfish arguments for marrying Agellius, she counters her brother's claim that a mere breath will separate him from his Christianity by becoming serious about the value of this very religion. The weariness of life would be bearable. This state of mind kept her from accepting what Aristo thought was a reasonable rebuttal as reasonable.

In Chapter XI, we learn with what seriousness Newman took both marriage and the religious life as commitments but likewise how he could enter into the demands of sharing one's inner life with others. The introduction to Agellius' proposal is reminiscent of the poignant section of the **Apologia** where he tells of the revolution of his mind and shortly after he recounted the death to paganism with Callista in terms similar to those on death to Anglicanism. The flowers become a series of symbols for Callista; ultimately, "not for a bridal wreath, but for a funeral urn."[38]

This meaning came because earlier a Christian slave of hers, Chione, had shared a dream of flowers which indicated her forthcoming death. By this challenge of Agellius' motivation in hoping Callista would marry him as she became a Christian, she forced him to lay bare his state of mind.

Just as the great revolution of mind brought Newman to share his most intimate thoughts and feelings so the revelation of Agellius' state of mind caused Callista to share her deepest self. She brought the narcissism and inconsistency of Agellius to the fore by her preaching with great earnestness what she had hoped of him. He could have, instead of using God for his purposes, taught her the present meaning of Christianity as Chione's example did. He could have replaced her dreary experience of paganism with a dedicated experience of his Risen Lord. Instead he joined with Aristo and Jucundus to expect her to lower him rather than to have him raise her. At the moment her state of mind was that of death: "She was absorbed in her own misery in an intense sense of degradation, in a keen consciousness of the bondage of nature, in a despair of ever finding what alone could give meaning to her existence, and an object to her intellect and affections."[39] Agellius responded with a conscience made tender by exposure. Newman observed the contrast: "the complaint of nature unregenerate . . . the self-reproach of nature regenerate and lapsing."[40]

Chapter XII seemed steeped in Newman's various illnesses. Agellius, shaken by the rejection and the exposure, bared himself to the overpowering noonday sun in a cloudless sky. A feverish daytime nightmare moved him to feel disdain for his weakness yet hope that his own martyrdom would regain his self-respect in Callista's eyes and in God's, when the outcast of Sicca caused him to read the decree against Christians. Rather than to seek out death, he slunk back to his cottage where a dizziness brought him to the ground.

Unaware of the confrontation, Jucundus rejoiced with word that Agellius had carried through on the proposal and hence concluded that his nephew's state of mind was such as Juba and he had suspected. Only Agellius' habit of stubbornness which Juba testified to worried Jucundus at the start of the persecution. Agellius might compulsively put himself in the way of the edict regardless of his state of mind towards Christianity. Here Newman took a moment out to remind us that Callista's better feelings were brought out in the confrontation, but that usually she was as resigned to her heathen background as the rest. At least this seemed to be her ordinary state of mind. Then he continued with the death of Agellius' past life, before, in the next chapter, bringing him back to life by the ministrations of Cyprian. Saying the Lord's Prayer and the Psalms, the two entered into his earlier failures as a mediocre Christian. By examining the relationship between early baptism and penance, Cyprian and he cooperated in Agellius' renewal. Fearing hell and his eternal loss, he hoped a second baptism were available or he would prefer to live a life where baptism was withheld until the time of death. Cyprian showed the narcissism of such a tact before providing penance as the way to a remedy.

Agellius' state of mind changed step by step through his convalescence from death to life, but Juba's confrontation with Cyprian highlighted the contrast. Juba called his pride - dignity; his pain at wrong doing the result of God forcing a conscience upon him; and haughtiness a singleness of purpose. Cyprian warned him that it was a sign that the fall was imminent and the voice was a warning. Agellius was not up to the confrontation and so sent his brother away. Before getting out of range of ear, Juba heard of the Good Shepherd, but his pact with evil caused him to shut his ears to Cyprian's encouragement. Suddenly Juba led Agellius and the priest to look up towards the scourge of locusts.

Chapter XV displayed Newman's fruits of years of meditation on Moses and the plagues on the Egyptians. For two chapters, Newman described the state of mind of the mob infuriated at the locust plague, but unable to determine how to use its energy and anger. Finally, coming upon a fine African ass after passing a lion, the crowd, moved by "the stimulus of famine and pestilence . . . added hatred of Christianity"[41] sought a Christian. Stage by stage the make up of the crowd increased in complexity and fullness until "the frenzied host, which progressed slowly through the streets, while every now and then, when there was an interval in the hubbub, the words **'Christianos ad leones'** were thundered out by some ruffian voice, and a thousand others fiercely regrouped."[42] One excuse followed the next in their search for a Christian until finally one who had been "punished with just severity . . . and (who) . . . had always cherished a malignant hatred . . . pointed out to the infuriated rabble the secluded mansion where the Christian household dwelt."[43] Yet the call against the Christians was merely a cover for the greed and hunger of the crowd. More devastating than the locust was the surging mob pushing through the wealthier section of Sicca.

Nonetheless they slaughtered the Christian cook of a wealthy Greek and then someone shouted, "Agellius, the Christian! Agellius the sorcerer! Agellius to the lions!" On to his cottage the crowd hurries. The principle behind the plague was the need for prayer and penance, but the result of the plague was a renewed attack upon Christians. A changed state of mind, indeed, but so far from its aim!

When Cyprian and Agellius parted after the long term teaching the former had given the latter, Newman gave more of the state of mind of Cyprian to the reader. His prayer was largely one of intercession - a prayer of one who knew the needs of so much of the Church. Upon the completion of his prayer of intercession, Cyprian slipped into contemplation as he adored the Eucharist.

Methods of thought enter once again with a discussion of hell. Agellius had feared hell enough to want to put off baptism, which he had already received, until death at the cost of not witnessing and living in God's presence through his own life. At that time Cyprian moved the question from a notional perspective to a real one, but even more firmly did he do this with Callista: "Suppose I understand you to say that you will never believe that **you** will go to an eternal Tartarus."[44] Her experiences of God's goodness and mercy and justice is hers to witness; as for others he has no way to know. Only after her own knowledge from personal experience will she be in a position to move to the knowledge of others.

Cyprian contrasts a variety of methods of thought. She had asserted she could not believe. She need not assent to opinion, however fact is another matter. It is a fact she has from her experience that she has been growing in unhappiness for a long period of time. Her earlier weariness with life revealed this state of mind Cyprian is now more fully uncovering;

while uncovering what her state of mind will be after death. Here something can give her surcease for moments, there "You will be yourself, shut up in yourself."[45]

Terrified by his disclosure of the teaching on hell, unsatisfied with the reality of Christ, Callista moved from thought to feelings so a fuller understanding of her state of mind would occur. Cyprian was forced to counter her Greek experience and state of mind with his Roman experience and state of mind. She as he, needed a conversion beyond these. This was not yet to be for she demanded perfection of Cyprian or of anyone who would convert her. As Juba **warned** of the locusts, Callista **warned of** the mob to come to take Agellius and Cyprian.

In Chapter XXV Newman finally goes beyond Jucundus' and Juba's account of Callista's state of mind as well as earnest preaching to Agellius to her own, yet to do so he had to contrast the states of mind of the crude Canaanites, the local constable, and Calphurnius. Each had a set of prejudices against the others. While each knew the weaknesses of the others in face of the edict! Always open to techniques of survival, their state of mind proved futile for pushing their own case. Also before describing Callista's state of mind, Newman showed more of Aristo's and then something of Cornelius'. As Polemo will be a specimen of the philosopher involved in such a time, Cornelius is to be a specimen of the pompous bureaucrat, officious and limited to the facts separated from meaning. Thus Newman entitled the experience of those planning to free Callista - "What Is the Meaning of It?"

Hence, Newman began Chapter XXVII - Am I a Christian? - with the question, "What was the state of mind of one who excited such keen interest in the narrow circle within which she was known?" . . . "And how does it differ from what it was some weeks before?"[46] Here Newman examined the growth of her state of mind from its seed. In concentric circles she went over the few truths she knew unable to answer objections, but aware these were mere difficulties which would disappear. She could but repeat what was told her by a few Christians and that she believed. Their statements were the extent of her knowledge and the "growth of her acceptance of it."[47] What gave sustenance to her belief was the disparity, yet unity of these witnesses in contrast to the confusion and emptiness of past religions she had come upon in Sicca. In place of a philosophy she had an Object to worship! One to speak to and with. An "intimate Divine Presence in her heart." Once she had gone beyond this common general impression her three Christian witnesses had shared with her, she could form a significant creed. This creed was constantly before her despite the difficulties and the dangers it posed. Their personal influence increased as she recognized that they possessed a common state of mind which she as yet lacked. They had a "simplicity, a truthfulness, a decision, an elevation, a calmness, and a sanctity."

Her change became obvious upon her imprisonment. The separation from the business of life freed her for the contemplation she had unknowingly sought by freeing herself from the boring demands of the world.

Aristo's state of mind, unchanged, could not apprehend Callista's changed state of mind so his hopes of being a savior were dashed by her willingness to be a martyr, but neither she nor he grasped this as yet. Polemo must be given an opportunity to change her state of mind before Cyprian finally secured her as a witness to Christianity. Polemo, as a specimen of the philosopher, actually portrayed the mind of a rhetorician in search of a feminine disciple. Hence, his revelation of his empty mind is in sharpest contrast with the personal influence of Cyprian.

All Callista could answer to the polemic of Polemo was her not being on "a scale of assent" at all. Only her conscience could speak and in reply she could claim, "I will not give up what I have, because I have not more." As the next chapter opened, Newman having entitled it "Conversion," began by noting the forlorn state of Callista's mind between atheism, as he considered paganism to be, and Christianity. This state of mind recalled his own death to Anglicanism before his rebirth to Catholicism highlighted in the **Apologia**: "Why don't you come faster? . . . because it takes time." So in this chapter he gave his main character time by contrasting the shallowness of Aristo and the depth of Jucundus. Yet with all of his seeming depth of love, Jucundus showed by accepting Calphurnius' help with Septimius that truth was not a real worth to him.

While waiting for a decision, Callista's hesitant state of mind during this period of conversion was shown by her neglect of the treasure Cyprianus had entrusted to her before his capture and escape - the Gospel of Luke. Deeper and deeper Newman entered into her state of mind as he questioned her variety of reasons for not reading this beautiful account of Jesus and the Church.[48] Through the use of this tender and awe inspiring writing, Newman expressed the "tension and suspense" of Callista's experience. On the one hand, she felt her sinfulness, on the other, his mercy. Thus, "by degrees, Callista began to walk by a new philosophy." But more important than the principles and methods of thought this conversion opened to her was Christ himself, who "exemplified all this wonderful philosophy."[49]

Meeting his one time servant, Aspar, as he fulfilled Cyprian's directions, Agellius rejoiced at the coincidence and provided the reader with Newman's acceptance of Providence in the signs these coincidences manifested.

The symbol of Plato's **Republic** continued - the sun of Africa - helpful especially to Callista, yet even to Juba. Whereas the Greek pride left Callista's face upon the conversion, in a lesser way it departed from Juba's. This defiance of Rome, a state of mind Newman recognized as the spirit of the world lacking peace, came forth as Callista finished her initiation into Christianity. No more hesitation could occur as the need to destroy Christianity in destroying Callista became clear to Rome. In face of this defiance Callista was ready for "she had passed through doubt, anxiety, perplexity, despondency, passion; but now she was in peace."[50] To enable us to feel this peace, Newman raised his symbol of light by his bold use of Apocalypse 12: a woman clothed with the sun: as Callista dreamed and experienced the sun drenched Greece she became aware of a woman "arranged more brilliantly than an oriental queen . . . the face changed . . . It had an innocence in its look . . . which bespoke both Maid and Mother."[51] Thus Newman recounted an early apparition of the Blessed Virgin Mary; "the light of Divinity now seemed to come through. Next the pierced side and feet of her savior brought the same to her. Then she heard that a Shepherd had found her."

The symbol of light and her homeland was really of her eternal homeland, but before it she experienced the darkness of her prison. Still on the morning of her martyrdom before light came from the sun, she exclaimed, "'O beautiful Light. . . . O Lovely Light, my light and my life.'"[52]

Agellius, in coming to retrieve Callista's body, meditates on the shattering before the new body she will be. He can bring out Him whom Cyprian can celebrate saying "**Lux Perpetua Sanctis Tuis, Domine.**"

Now to review what we have found in the **Grammar**. When we consider
the purposes of Newman in writing the **Grammar**, it is necessary to state
that the key principle is on page 140 ff. Here he asks "whether there is
such an act of the mind as assent at all." This question brings out a series
of examples of Newman's acumen in the use of rhetoric. His audience is
formed from those who have grown up on Locke and Hume; one part is his preferred audience: believers in God and eternal judgment; the other part is
his antagonistic audience, an audience which puts unlettered believers in
a defensive position.

Probably the most outstanding rhetorical effort in the **Grammar** has
to do with the distinction and what enters into distinction between inference
and assent on pages 140-148. This can be divided into two specimens, however
it will be helpful to begin with the question of states of mind on page
147. "There is only one sense in which we are allowed to call such acts
or states of mind assents. They are opinions; and, as being such, they
are, as I have already observed, when speaking of Opinion, assents to the
plausibility, probability, doubtfulness, or untrustworthiness, of a proposition; that is, **not variations of assent to an inference, but assents to
a variation in inferences.** When I assent to a doubtfulness, or to a probability, my assent, as such, is **as complete as if I** assented to a truth; it
is not a certain degree of assent."

This paragraph summarizes the issues of the two specimens and prepares
for the conclusion. Earlier, on pages 60 ff. and 64 ff., he had given,
as part of the grammar of assent, definitions of credence and opinion.
Those trained in the thought of John Locke and David Hume could easily read
degrees of assent into those definitions. Here Newman rebuts the **a priori**

theory of inference and assent by a careful distinction between variation of assent and variations in inferences. The conditional and unconditional aspects of our thinking stand out clearly in this distinction. The methods of thought of these pages match the excellence of Newman's rhetoric.

Rhetorically, Newman begins the treatment of the **an sit** question with hypotheses contrary to fact:

"if a professed act can only be viewed

  as the necessary and immediate repetition of another act,

  if assent is a sort of a reproduction or a double of another act,

  if when inference determines that

  a proposition is

  somewhat, or not a little, or a good deal, or very like

  truth,

      assent as its natural and normal counterpart says

  that it **is**

  somewhat, or not a little, or a good deal, or very like

  truth,

  then I do not see. . . . It is simply superfluous, in the

  psychological point of view, and a curiosity for subtle minds."

In these instances, Newman is recalling the English mind which dissuades its authors from subtleties and from redundancy.

If assent is a mere redundancy, then

"When I assent, I am supposed . . . to do precisely

           what I do when I infer,

  or rather not quite so much,

  but something which is included in inferring;

  for, while the disposition of my mind (another way of saying states of mind) toward a given proposition is

identical in assent and in inference,

I merely drop the thought of the premises when I assent,

though not of their influence on the proposition inferred."

Obviously, Newman, in presenting the case for the opposition, grasps the arguments Locke and Hume have repeated, and which Gilson missed in his reading, and which we will present immediately after this summary specimen.

Next Newman brings up the **supposedly** parallel case: "that an act of conscious recognition, though distinct from an act of knowledge, is after all only its repetition." This favorite method of thought in Newman is denied here and further **rebutted**: "such a recognition is a reflex act with its own object." Thus he distinguishes the acts by their objects, which should have been simple enough for Gilson and the followers of Locke and Hume to do. Finally, he comes to the principle. This is the opposite principle of Locke and Hume and therefore of his English audience. Either they are converted to this principle or the entire **Grammar** is a failure for them.

"Either assent is intrinsically distinct from inference, or the sooner we get rid of the word in philosophy the better." As an Englishman he wants no redundancy, but he also wants distinctions to have meaning. This principle leads him to a series of hypotheses which express the utter lack of identity between inference and assent:

"if it does not admit of being confused

if the two words are used for two operations of the intellect

if in matter of fact they are not always found together

if they do not vary with each other

if one is sometimes found without the other

if one is strong when the other is weak

if **sometimes** they seem even in conflict with each other

> then (which prepares us for the method of thought of parallel
>
> cases again)

since we know perfectly well what an inference is,"

> we must consider what assent is.

This type of consideration is experiential. Locke and Hume drove the English to distraction with their **a priori** approach which they called **a posteriori**. Newman could call his experiential, since he writes "as it is daily brought before us."

At this point in the rhetoric, it is sobering to recall Seymour Sarason's epilogue to **Psychology and Mental Retardation**:

> The narrowness of our view has the virtue of rendering experience meaningful and justifying our actions (no small virtue!), and it has the vice (no small vice!) of making humbleness and respect for complexity conspicuous by their absence. The need to believe that our view is the true one maximizes, among other things, polarizations, controversies, and even wars.[1]

Following upon Sarason's epilogue, we find that Newman looked upon the universe and recognized how difficult it would be to find God if it were not for faith. Elsewhere he expounds upon the many limits of his thought, yet he wrote the **Grammar** to achieve certitude.

The specimen, then, which most fully and compendiously provides the purpose of the **Grammar** is the opening of the treatment of Complex Assent on pages 157-158.

"I have been considering assent

as the mental assertion of an intelligible proposition,

as an act of the intellect direct, absolute,

complete in itself, unconditional, arbitrary,

yet not incompatible with an appeal to argument,

and at least in many cases exercised unconsciously.
On this last characteristic of assent

I have not insisted,

as it has not come in my way;

nor is it more than an accident of acts of assent,

though an ordinary accident.

That it is of ordinary occurrence cannot be doubted.

A great many of our assents are merely expressions of our

personal likings, tastes, principles, motives, and

opinions, as dictated by nature, or resulting from habit;

in other words, they are acts and manifestations of self:

now what is more rare than self-knowledge?

In proportion then to our ignorance of self,

is our unconsciousness of those innumerable acts of assent,

which we are incessantly making. And so again

in what may be almost called the mechanical operation of

our minds,

in our continual acts of apprehension and inference,

speculation, and resolve, propositions pass before us and

receive our assent without our consciousness.

Hence it is that we are so apt to confuse together

acts of assent and acts of inference. Indeed, I may fairly

say, that those assents which we give with a direct

knowledge of what we are doing, are few compared with the

multitude of like acts which pass through our minds in long

succession without our observing them.

That mode of assent which is exercised thus unconsciously, I

may call simple assent, and of it I have treated in the
foregoing section; but now I am going to speak of such
assents as must be made consciously and deliberately, and
which I call complex or reflex assents. And I begin by
recalling what I have already stated about the relation in
which Assent and Inference stand to each other,
Inference, which holds propositions conditionally, and
Assent, which unconditionally accepts them; the relation is
this:
Acts of Inference are both the antecedents of assent before
assenting, and its usual concomitants after assenting. For
instance, I hold absolutely that the country which we call
India exists, upon trustworthy testimony; and next, I may
continue to believe it on the same testimony. In like
manner, I have ever believed that Great Britain is an
island, for certain sufficient reasons; and on the same
reasons I may persist in the belief."

"But it may happen that I forget my reasons for what I believe to be
so absolutely true; or I may never have asked myself about them, or formally
marshalled them in order, and have accustomed to assent without a recognition
on my assent or of its grounds, and then perhaps something occurs which
leads to my reviewing and completing those grounds, analyzing and arranging
them, yet without on that account implying of necessity any suspense, ever
so slight, of assent, to the proposition that India is in a certain part
of the earth, and that Great Britain is an island.

"With no suspense of assent at all; any more than the boy in my former
illustration had any doubt about the answer set down in his arithmetic book,

when he began working out the question; any more than he would be doubting his eyes and his common sense, that the two sides of a triangle are together greater than the third, because he drew out the geometrical proof of it. He does but repeat, after his formal demonstration, that assent which he made before it, and assents to his previous assenting. This is what I call a reflex or complex assent.

". . . there is no necessary incompatibility between thus assenting and yet proving, - for the conclusiveness of a proposition is not synonymous with its truth."

This specimen clarifies the reasons we confuse assents and inferences. It also clarifies the major distinction between inquiry and investigation through which the relationship of the state of mind and methods of thought become clear. This is the prime example of Newman's method of thought by the use of definition.

Day by day we come upon people who are surprised that others assent to what they do and this without argument. Involved in their surprise is their dismay that the person is merely asserting without giving any reason for the assertion. At the same time, the matter is open to a number of excellent arguments. For instance, a group of students of metaphysics gradually argue to the fact of existence. They glow as they share this insight with a fellow classmate who is as capable as they and who usually is as willing as they to enter into the labyrinth of argument. Suddenly their classmate takes them back with his assertion that it is too obvious that he exists to spend any time or thought in arguing the point. Their warm contentment at the end of their struggle seems more important than their assent to their existence. His assertion seems to be the result of mere unconscious awareness. They push him to enter into the inference with them.

He agrees this would be to some extent better if he were to convince another, but at this time, for him, it is a sheer waste.

Or, again, before exchange of vows, friends of the bride-to-be come to argue with her over her decision. They have brought a variety of arguments pro and con which might have worried Desdemona. She, like Desdemona, finds no need to enter into the inferences. Her assertion of her love is adequate. Any argument would add nothing to her reasons for loving Othello.

Or, again, was Job better off before his three friends came with their arguments than after he went beyond them? Or, was he better off after his argument with God? Was not his simple assertion enough?

Or, finally, "By this shall all men know you love me, if you have love for one another." Here the act is the assertion. The assent is obvious from its results.

In each case, we find "acts and manifestations of self" in these simple assents. What the questioners want is more than simple assent. They want an argument; an inference. The results would be self-knowledge. However most of us lack self-knowledge. We take the basis of our assents for granted. We are satisfied with the fact that things are as they are. Instead of entering into the reasons, we live our lives on our assents.

These assents then can be due to "our personal likings, (those tendencies which a recent singer gave notoriety in the words, "it feels so right"), tastes, principles, (those starting points which enable us to move from what we have been given to operation), motives, (impulses within which we find the basis for acting in accord with our tendencies), and opinions (through which we go beyond mere credence to the pros and cons of our actions), as dictated by nature, or resulting from habit."

Plato concluded in the **Meno** that there are three ways to knowledge: by nature, by teaching, or by gift. Here Newman is not ready to go to the gift, but his reason for not doing so is given on page 156: "Assent is ever assent; but in the assent which follows a divine announcement, and is vivified by a divine grace, there is, from the nature of the case, a transcendent adhesion of mind, intellectual and moral, and a special self-protection, beyond the operation of those ordinary laws of thought, which alone have a place in my discussion."

We do not know ourselves in these unconscious acts. We act and our sources can be obvious to those about us, but we ourselves lack the consciousness. Our state of mind, in other words, is not that of self-knowledge, but outside of certitude and reasonable justification. What we take for granted is sufficient justification.

We are, Newman stresses, in a mechanical state of mind towards "our continual acts of apprehension and inference, speculation, and resolve, propositions pass before us and receive our assent without our consciousness." In such a state of mind, we are unprepared to distinguish inference and assent. The flow from one to the other is confused. One starts and ends; the other starts and ends, but where the starting point and ending of each or either is, is beyond our consciousness. It is enough to assert and to act. What was behind our assertion does not bother us and why we act does not. What is important is to live our daily lives.

Jean Piaget made this case with a pair of young children. As they walked they watched the moon. From hints in the conversation it was evident that they were having the experience of the moon moving with them. He placed one child at a particular spot and walked the other to a spot some fifteen yards away. He took a position between them and commanded them to come to him. When they arrived he asked the children who had come from opposite directions to tell him the direction of the moon's movement. When they gave contrary statements, he confronted them with the inconsistency. Before they were free to take the moon's motion for granted. Henceforth they were required to go beyond their relative positions. They moved a bit towards self-knowledge. Piaget realized that few of us would make many steps without the confrontation of our peers.

Newman had already stated his position: "those assents which we give with direct knowledge of what we are doing, are few." We unconsciously make simple assents instead of consciously and deliberately making complex assents.

Inferences are conditionally held propositions; assents are unconditionally accepted propositions. They are related as follows: "Acts of inference are both the antecedents of assent before assenting, and its usual concomitants after assenting."

This issue was well described by James Collins in "The Heart's Way to God: Newman and the Assent to God" in **God and Modern Philosophy**. "Is the certitudinal assent to God a simple or a reflex one, a notional or a real one?"[2] Whereas he agrees with the last page of the **Grammar** where Newman unites the four, Etienne Gilson claims the opposite. Gilson avoids pages 145, 158, and 379. Newman on these pages reveals the complexity of human knowing. We act imaginatively in religion; intellectually in theology; generally in our notional assent; personally in our real assent.

Before we accept the pursuit we reason (usually and logically), then we assent to the pursuit. We next return to the reasoning. What has so convinced us should convince others. We must examine the proposition. Its "conclusiveness . . . is not synonymous with its truth." What state of mind did this achievement of conclusiveness bring me to? How did the method of thought participate in this achievement? How did the principles I hold enter into it? How did the antecedent reasonings prepare me? Over and over again, we find that before we assent and after we assent we have the experience of inquiry and investigation. That is, if we have a certain education and a certain **noblesse oblige**, if we find that our assent as simple is inadequate for our station, we realize, as the **Oxford University Sermons** put it: "we must give a reason for the hope which is in us. The implicit reason is not enough. We must find and give the explicit reason."[3]

Principles/ States of Mind

Here again the issues of this work come together. But here we find the difficulty those who follow Thomas Aquinas originally have along with Gilson. Seemingly we cannot at the same time know and believe. And to assent seems to be equivalent to believe and to know is to demonstrate. Yet Newman distinguishes logic and informal inference. Rather than enter into the debate, it is good to take the antecedent reasoning Newman suggests and follow Leslie Stephen who catches the distinction Newman made.

Here then we find that pursuing the tools of this work we come upon a number of critical issues. Rather than expecting to solve all of these issues, we prefer to expect to fashion a number of **status quaestionis**. And already we find how Newman would have us operate. We do not give up the certitude we have that there is a compatibility of the four assents in returning to grasp why Gilson would deny their compatibility. Instead we would merely take it for granted that "to contemplate (a proposition) under one aspect, is not to contemplate it under another; and the two aspects may be consistent, from the very fact that they are two **aspects**."[4]

Though the **Essay on the Development of Christian Doctrine** is not one of the writings from which a large selection of specimens has been taken for this work; yet Chapter V, Section II, n. 3 on principles is of great help for the issue of opinion as well as that of states of mind, principles, and methods of thought. "A development, to be faithful, must retain both the doctrine and the principle with which it started."[5] "Without doctrine, a principle is fruitless. Its vitality springs from its interaction with doctrine; and on the other hand, a principle lacking doctrine is really the state of religious minds in the heathen world." The principle does not determine its direction. One can go either towards atheism or towards God. Here we find the position Newman will build **Loss and Gain** upon; the position which will show up in the **Apologia**; the position which will be most fully cared for in the **Grammar**. As he here put it:

> This, too, is often the solution of the paradox 'Extremes meet,' and of the startling reactions which take place in individuals; viz., the presence of some one principle condition, which is dominant in their minds from first to last. If one of two contradictory alternatives be necessarily true on a certain hypothesis, then the denial of the one leads, by mere logical consistency and without direct reasons, to a reception of the other.[6]

There is then no midway, no stopping point, between the movement of the principle without doctrine towards faith and away from it. It is an either/or situation.

But what of a person with a principle but without a fully developed doctrine? In the beginning of the **Apologia**, Newman uses Hurrell Froude as such an example. In Newman's path, how did Froude have an influence? He found him seemingly effervescent. Each idea sprang with a stimulating vitality from his mouth. But before these ideas came forth, they took a toll on Froude. "Dying prematurely, as he did, and in the conflict and transition-state of opinion, his religious views never reached their ultimate conclusion, by the very reason of their multitude and their depth."

Hence these ideas did not bring Newman to certitude, but to a changed state of opinion. He readily sought out both principles and doctrines to pair with these. Four of these pairings had a great impact on Newman: "He taught me to look with admiration towards the Church of Rome, and in the same degree to dislike the Reformation. He fixed deep in me the idea of devotion to the Blessed Virgin, and he led me gradually to believe in the Real Presence."[7]

This specimen indicates that our states of mind and our principles can be molded by those who have not yet found the completion of their own. The interaction of searching minds which will play a crucial role in the **Idea** is here recalled in the first third of Newman's life. Keble shaped Froude and Froude did as much as anyone to shape Newman. We should not be surprised therefore, at the end of the Discourse VII to read Crabbe's poetry: "To fashion a philosophy and a poetry of his own."

The same significance of principle in Newman becomes demonstratively before us in the next period: 1833-1839 where he gives us his states of mind and principles on pages 44-46. "From the age of fifteen, dogma has been the fundamental principle of my religion. . . . What I held in 1816, I held in 1833, and I hold in 1864. Please God, I shall hold it to the end."

The significance of this principle cannot be over-stated. The basis against which he judged the Liberalism of his day, which was his constant antagonist, was this principle. In the **Development** essay he lists his principles and this is the crucial one. Just as here he rooted his belief in "a visible Church, with sacraments and rites which are the channels of invisible grace,"[8] so there he gave the basis for holding that the Church was the same in Antiquity, in the time of the Reformation, and in his day. This same three-fold movement is clear. His third principle was that of authority residing in his bishop. These explicit principles pervade Newman and only where states of mind and principles are found in the same specimen will we examine them because they are truly involved in everything.

The state of mind which Newman examined in its changing conditions twice in the **Grammar** showed itself tied to principle. As the state of mind appeared to dissolve, in fact, it remained the same through a series of transformations.

Early in the **Apologia** we find a graduated scale of assents. In the **Grammar**, we find there is no scale of assents. Instead, either we assent or we do not assent. Hence we are faced with a dilemma: the **Apologia** is an account of Newman's history of religious opinion and the **Grammar** is an account of how others exhibit their religious and ethical assents. The former is shown also in **Loss and Gain**; the latter is shown in **Callista**. The issue in each seems to be a graduated scale: from atheism to Christianity, but the issue is really about states of mind. Once we change our focus from a scale of assents to states of mind we realize we can have a graduated scale without confusion over the conditional and the unconditional. Newman handled this dilemma well. A documentation of his handling will save us from confusion.

The clarification of the issue is contained in Note 2 of the **Grammar**. Both Newman and his friend were aware of the way out of the confusion concerning the relation between atheism, Catholicism, and evidence. All four of these works make the varieties of evidence for religion obvious, yet readers unprepared for comparing states of mind could miss the point.

Newman's defender and Newman himself were prepared.

The **Grammar** is rife with examples of his clarity on states of mind as is **Callista**. We will begin with the latter. **Callista** examines each character's states of mind in relation to atheism and Christianity, or paganism and Catholicity. In the first chapters, we find a contrast between the states of mind of the pagan and a lukewarm Christian. Two brothers, Juba and Agellius represent these varying states. Juba is stuck in the door of the Church. Agellius has barely entered. Juba is unaware of his state of mind, while his brother assumes his state of mind is more fully Christian than it is. This state of mind is most important: for the novel and for the historical situation. If Agellius is truly of the state of mind of the Christian during a period of persecution, he is in danger for his faith. States of mind have consequences.

Digression on Purpose

James Strachey on page 3 of Volume 1 of the **Collected Papers** provided a warning as applicable to readers of John Henry Newman as of Freud: "The only really satisfactory way of acquiring a knowledge of Professor Freud's writings is to follow the order of development of his work."[9] This is the case Jean Stern, Maurice Nedoncelle, and others have made for Newman, but just as most will not read the five volumes of Freud's work, so most will not read all of Newman. Thus we are led back to James Collins' introduction to **Philosophical Readings in Cardinal Newman** where he warns us: "It is better at the outset to assimilate a few basic themes in Newman than to attempt a fast expedition through all his writings. . . . In the second place, it is safer for us to focus upon Newman's own text studied for its own sake. We can accept the paradox that Newman's contemporary relevance lies precisely in being himself and inviting us to study his thought in its own shape and texture."[10]

By coincidence, Stephen Gould was reviewing Rudwick's masterful treatment of the Devonian resolution to the Buckland, Sedgwick, and Murchison controversy for the **New York Review of Books** as I organized the present work February 9, 1986. His chief criticism was structural. Rudwick used a strictly developmental narrative style. This put the reader in the same state of confusion as the investigators, but at what cost? Gould knew the answer so he could follow the narrative. He also realized that as admirable as Rudwick's intention and his use of the narrative style to avoid distortion, there was a way to preserve the style while yet not distorting. Just as Gould found examples of how to do this, in like manner he expected Rudwick equally capable.

The point of these comments is that those readers who lack the luxury of reading everything Newman wrote and reading it in the order in which he came upon the ideas need a valid approach to Newman much more economical and far less confusing. This is the purpose of the present work. There are several themes which had a significant interest for Newman that are better understood today, yet which reveal the reader's need for continued study. These have been followed not in a strictly chronological order, but in the order of interest for Newman and hence for us.

The themes which go through all the writings of Newman which have been selected are atheism, methodology, and direction. Atheism became agnosticism from the early days of liberalism; methodology became psychology of assent from the early days of implicit and explicit reason and its later presentation as the grammar of assent; and direction became conversion from its original history of his religious opinions.

These three themes give a unity to the present work, but similarly the use of principles, states of mind, and methods of thought give it a unity. Each specimen from Newman's writings has been chosen on the two-fold criteria of these themes and as an example of his use of these three parts of his methodology. Once the reader comes to this point, it will be possible to continue the exercise not only into all of Newman's writings, but into the writings of present day authors.

Reading a novel with these in mind enables one to notice the characters, the action, and the plot in themselves and in the approach the author has taken. In reading an essay, the problem at issue becomes clear through these. In deciphering a letter, one is able to determine the unity or lack of unity in the missive. And so on with other genres.

When faced with an unsynthesized complex thinker, it is tempting to oversimplify. To avoid oversimplification, we recognized from the start that we have been merely attempting to apply a method of approach to specimens of Newman's writings. The reader can determine whether the method increases **aporiae** and the move towards understanding. As a revealer of **aporiae**, does the method highlight issues which should be faced? Do these issues and their setting or context move one towards understanding?

Most of the use of the method has to be excluded for the reasons of space and interest. As the method was developed, more and more sections of Newman seemed appropriate, but this would have been redundant. Readers are able to find Newman's works easily. The interest of the reader is primary. We know that the further we go in our search for wisdom, the more we appreciate the value of method and in certain periods, we enjoy method for its own sake, yet until we reach a true respect for method we find it can put us off. Nonetheless the content we are able to master is in proportion to our control of method. Interest continues and grows as we develop methods which reveal the newness of what exists. Any revelation to others is limited by their control of method.

On the way to the interest of method, we find the need for **aporiae.** Unless we can make our search a burning question for others they will not accept the journey. They will not go up so they cannot go down. And those who are unwilling to teach others the way up will reap the harvest of those who are willing to satisfy the curiosity of those who are unwilling to learn method.

However the usual way to convince another that the way is worth the effort is to reveal the end immediately. In this search, we have come upon the end in Newman, then in James Collins, and finally in Karl Rahner. At page 379 of the **Grammar,** we were told the results of Newman's gathering of specimens; in Collins we find "in the synthesis between the informal inference from conscience and the four kinds of assent, Newman finds his fundamental natural answer to the problem of modern atheism and philosophical naturalism which he so vividly appreciated and which underlies all his investigations."[11]

Rahner begins his preface for **Pastoral Approach to Atheism:** "no question is more important and topical for the Church today than the question of how to approach the problem of atheism spiritually and pastorally."[12]

In writing **Utilitarianism,** Stephen provided the epitome of antecedent probability contrast. If one is agnostic and atheistic, then assumptions Newman made are unacceptable. And Newman frequently stressed that if we find an opponent will not accept our principle, and we both understand the meaning of each other's words, then there is no real purpose in continuing the discussion which will become merely polemical.

For this reason, in writing to Newman over the differences on certitude, Froude claimed: "I have already said that I do not venture to enter into controversy with you, but yet there are one or two things which your letter impels me to try to say in reference to it."[13]

In the latter letter, Froude made it obvious how one can offer the value of witness to those with whom one differs:

> The **Apologia** has been very much read by men of Science and with a feeling of great interest, a feeling which couples the perception of extreme power of mind in the writer with an anxious and (wondering) curiosity to know how he substantiates the bridge by which he steps so freely from the state of doubt which (as they feel) inevitably attaches to these results of probabilities, to the state of absolute certainty which he seems to substitute for this. I travelled with Sir C. Lyell the other day to London on his return from the British Association Meeting at Bath, and without my leading the conversation in that direction the subject came naturally to the surface and he expressed the feeling which I have mentioned not indeed as having a misgiving that you would be able to turn the stream back but as knowing that what you have to say would deserve very serious consideration.[14]

Newman and Froude understood the influence the former had. Even though they knew Liberalism was to have its day, there would always be that gnawing doubt - that Newman did not go along with them.

How deeply his departure from Oxford hurt him, knowing then what he and Froude and Lyell knew, the power of his influence. Then it might have turned the stream, now it could only force it from running over everything in its path.

With this understanding in mind, Newman had written "Christianity and Scientific Investigation." Later he would prepare his acceptance speech - his bigiletto - on the influence of Liberalism. In the earlier, he would warn of the dangers of scientific investigation without fearing them; in the latter he would accept the inevitable and tell of how to take the good from the evil, just as his predecessor, St. Basil, had taught the Greek teachers not to fear the poison of the plants, but as bees separate out the good.

Visual Analysis of Concluding Specimens of the **Grammar**
Methods of Thought
Conclusion of the **Grammar**

Newman's **Grammar** has a pattern of four chapters of definitions and distinctions followed by a chapter of application. The first pattern is on apprehension and assent, and the second is on inference and assent. These terms are in the tradition of the English thinkers. The first pattern concludes with the issue of the One God and the Triune God. The second concludes with a series of specimens on Natural Religion and Revealed Religion.

The importance of these two application chapters, 5 and 10, prepares the reader for an exceptionally developed and completely organized set of arguments. Newman does not disappoint the reader. Four outstanding specimens will justify this claim: "Supreme Being," pages 93-98; "Conscience," 98-101; "Natural Religion," 323-324; and "Mediation of Christ," 375-376, 379.

"Supreme Being" is an argument which carefully distinguishes the proof for the existence of God and the grounds for such a proof from the characteristics of God once the existence of God is granted. The preamble of the argument and the use of conscience as assumed make up the content of these sections from Chapter 5.

The audience taken negatively and positively is the content of "Natural Religion," the first section selected from Chapter 10. Newman first identifies the correct audience in order to feel at ease in assuming what he must so he can argue from the experience of his audience. The argument has its significance in preparing the reader for the necessary states of mind Revealed Religion calls for. The link between Chapter 5 becomes clear in the basis for the identification of these states of mind.

The principle involved is Butler's analogy. And the impact and the validity of these methods of thought, states of mind, and principles are obvious in the last pages of the **Grammar,** where Newman reveals the fact that once a person had finished the order of the argument as the needs of the audience required, one would be in a position to begin at the end and re-read the argument the other way. In other words, there is a **via inventionis** and a **via judicii.** Newman must follow the way of discovery with the reader before the reader is ready to return over the route with the discovery.

The principle Newman used is that which Aristotle discovered in drama and in the Analogy of the Cave. In recapitulating the latter, Aristotle recognized

that which is most intelligible in itself is

least intelligible to us

and that which is least intelligible in itself

is most intelligible to us.

We can profit most from Chapter 10 by re-reading it after finding the principle, but we need the order he followed to discover the principle and accept it.

With this preamble, we are ready for the specimens. Rather than merely printing them, we will present them in rhythm and structure for their full force as we have with Aristotle's principle.

a) "minds properly prepared for it . . .

b) I do not address . . ."

150

Then on pages 323 and following:

"I do not address myself to those,

who in moral evil and physical see nothing more than
imperfections of a parallel nature;

who consider that the difference in gravity between the
two is one of degree only, not of kind;

that moral evil is merely the offspring
of physical, and

that as we remove the latter so we inevitably
remove the former;

that there is a progress of the human race
which tends to the annihilation of moral evil;

that knowledge is virtue,

and vice is ignorance;

that sin is a bugbear, not a reality;

that the Creator does not punish
except in the sense of correcting;

that vengeance in Him would of necessity
be vindictiveness;

that all that we know of Him, be it much
or little, is through the laws of nature;

that miracles are impossible;

that prayer to Him is a superstition;

that the fear of Him is unmanly;

that the sorrow for sin is slavish and abject;

that the only intelligible worship of Him
is to act well our part in the world,

and the only sensible repentance

to do better in future;

that if we do our duties in this life,

we may take our chance for the next; and

that it is of no use perplexing our minds

about the future state,

for it is all a matter of guess.

These opinions characterize a civilized age; and if I say that I will not argue about Christianity with men who hold them, I do so,

not as claiming any right to be impatient or peremptory with

any one,

but because it is plainly absurd to attempt to prove

a second proposition to those

who do not admit the first.

I assume then that the above system of opinion is simply false, inasmuch as it contradicts the primary teachings of nature in the human race, wherever a religion is found and its workings can be ascertained.

I assume the presence of God in our conscience,

and the universal experience, as keen as our

experience of bodily pain,

of what we call a sense of sin or guilt.

This sense of sin, as of something not only evil in itself, but an affront to the good God, is chiefly felt as regards one or other of three violations of His law.

He Himself is	Against His Majesty are
Sanctity,	impurity,
Truth, and	inveracity, and

Love;   cruelty.

All men are not distressed at these offences alike;

   but the piercing pain and sharp remorse

      which one or other inflicts upon the mind,

         till habituated to them,

   brings home to it the notion of what sin is,

   and is the vivid type and representative

      of its intrinsic hatefulness.

Starting from these elements, we may determine without difficulty the class of sentiments, intellectual and moral, which constitute the formal preparation for entering upon what are called the Evidences of Christianity.

These evidences, then presuppose a belief and perception of the Divine Presence,

      a recognition of His attributes and

      an admiration of His Person viewed under them;

      a conviction of the worth of the soul and

         of the reality and momentousness of the

            unseen world,

      an understanding that, in proportion as we partake in

         our own persons of the attributes which we admire

            in Him,

               we are dear to Him;

         a consciousness on the contrary that we are far from

            exemplifying them,

      a consequent insight into our guilt and misery,

      an eager hope of reconciliation to Him,

a desire to know and to love Him, and

a sensitive looking-out in all that happens,

whether in the course of human nature or

human life,

for tokens, if such there be,

of His bestowing on us what we so

greatly need.

These are specimens of the state of mind for which I stipulate in those who would inquire into the truth of Christianity;

and my warrant for so definite a stipulation lies in the

teaching, as I have described it, of

conscience and the moral sense,

in the testimony of those religious rites

which have ever prevailed in all parts of

the world, and in the

character and conduct of those

who have commonly been

selected by the popular

instinct as the special

favourites of Heaven."

Next on pages 375 and following:

"I have been forestalling all along the thought with which I shall close considerations on the subject of Christianity;

and necessarily forestalling it,

because it properly comes first,

though the course which my argument has taken has not allowed me to introduce it in its natural place.

Revelation begins where Natural Religion fails.

The Religion of Nature is a mere inchoation,

and needs a complement,

--it can have but one complement,

and that very complement is

Christianity.

Natural Religion is based upon the sense of sin;

it recognizes the disease,

but it cannot find,

it does but look out for the remedy.

That remedy, both for guilt and moral impotence,

is found in the central doctrine of Revelation, the

Mediation of Christ.

. . . Christianity is the fulfillment of the promise made to

Abraham, and of the Mosaic revelations;

This is how it has been able from the first to

occupy the world and gain a hold on every class of

human society to which its preachers reached;

This is why the Roman power and the multitude of

religions which it embraced could not stand against it;

this is the secret of its sustained energy,

and its never-flagging martyrdoms;

this is how at present it is so mysteriously potent,

in spite of the new and fearful adversaries

which beset its path.

It has with it that gift of staunching and healing the one deep wound of

human nature,

which avails more for its success than a full encyclopedia of

scientific knowledge and a whole library of controversy,

and therefore it must last while human nature lasts.

It is a **living truth** which never can grow old.

Some persons speak of it as if it were a thing of history,

with only indirect bearings upon modern times;

I cannot allow that it is a mere historical religion.

Certainly it has its foundations in past and glorious

memories, but its power is in the present.

It is no dreary matter of antiquarianism;

we do not contemplate it in conclusions

drawn from dumb documents and dead events,

but by faith exercised in **ever-living** objects,

and by the appropriation and use of **ever-recurring** gifts.

Our communion with it is **in** the unseen,

not **in** the obsolete.

Upon the doctrines which I have mentioned as central truths,

others, as we all know,

follow,

which rule our personal conduct.

Here I end my specimens, among the many which might be given, of the arguments adducible for Christianity. I have dwelt upon them, in order to show how I would apply the principles of this Essay to the proof of its divine origin. Christianity is addressed, both as regards its evidences and its contents, to minds which are in the normal condition of human nature,

as believing in God and in a future judgement.

Such minds it addresses both through

the intellect and

the imagination;

 creating a certitude of its truth by arguments

  too various for direct enumeration,

  too personal and deep for words,

  too powerful and concurrent for refutation.

Nor need reason come first and faith second (though this is the logical order), but one and the same teaching is in different aspects both object and proof,

 and elicits one complex act both of inference and of assent.

 It speaks to us one by one, and

 it is received by us one by one,

  as the counterpart, so to say,

  of ourselves, and

   is real as we are real."

Grammar Misunderstood

 John Henry Newman's **An Essay in Aid of a Grammar of Assent** has been misunderstood frequently enough that Etienne Gilson, the famous historian of philosophy, introducing the work, devoted approximately half of his pages to indicating three of these misunderstandings: however, earlier, he had stated "As Newman always succeeds in making himself clear to those who have the patience to follow his explanations, we have not deemed it necessary to burden his text with commentaries."[15] Yet before outlining these three misinterpretations, Gilson seems to have added a new misinterpretation.

  Newman in no way denies that, most of the time,
the propositions to which our intellect assents are
offered to us as conclusions of some previous inference,

but he wants us to distinguish between: (1) the propositions which we accept, in the light of their demonstrations, as inferences; (2) the propositions which, because
we accept them for themselves, directly and no longer
in the light of any previous demonstrations, can be
said to be objects of assent properly so called. True
enough, a proposition first accepted as an inference
can become later on an object of assent. The point
is that where there is real assent, all traces of previous
reasonings, justifications, and demonstrations have
disappeared from the mind. No proposition can, at one
and the same time, be object of assent and object of
inference, Newman's assent is characterized by its unconditionality.[16]

This long quotation from Gilson was necessary to give him an opportunity

to present his position, but also due to the fact that his position even

as an objection provides a means for reading the **Grammar** more carefully

and intelligently. Searching for the pro and con of his presumed distinction,

we come to understand what Newman had in mind. Nor need we search alone,

as James Collins has come to some of the same issues from another vantage

point: the synthetic.

Gilson examines the acceptance of propositions in light of inference

and in light of assent. How are these related? Seemingly, propositions

which are accepted as a result of demonstrations are inferences. The process

of inference concludes in certainty due to the evidence of the demonstration.

Though this process prepares the way for the assent, when the assent is

made there is no longer any need for the inference. Gilson could have used

the specimens Newman collected to show why we need two terms: inference

and assent, rather than only one, inference, as justification for the distinc-

tions. Nonetheless, Newman is explicit in the first chapter that this dis-

tinction is not a separation. However, Gilson concludes his treatment by

requiring a separation of inference and assent and he bases this upon the

unconditionality of assent.

On page 27 we read: "Nay further, in all minds there is a certain co-existence of these distinct acts; that is, of two of them, for we can at once infer and assent. . . . Indeed, in a multitude of cases, we infer truths, or apparent truths, before, and while, and after we assent to them."[17]

At about this time, in the preface of the third edition of the **Oxford University Sermons,** Newman had given an example of this co-existence of inference and assent:

> Since, in accepting a conclusion, there is a virtual recognition of its premises, an act of Faith may be said (improperly) to include in it the reasoning process which is its antecedent, and to be in a certain aspect an exercise of Reason; and thus is co-ordinate, and in contrast, with the three (improper) senses of the word 'Reason' above enumerated, viz., explicit, evidential, and secular Reason.[18]

Here we have Newman using the term "virtual" in the sense of "in the power of" or "implicitly." In the sermon, Newman was struggling to grasp an explanation of assent as well as of faith. In this preface, he listed some 15 points of clarification. Because he had just published the **Grammar,** he was in a position to notice the meanings he would have wanted to have exposed more clearly before. As is so frequent with Newman, his later works and editions form an exegesis of his earlier works.

Though Gilson seems to have misinterpreted Newman, whom we can agree with or not depending upon our illative sense, he has a helpful explanation for misunderstanding: "One reason for this is the originality of his under-taking confronted with a strictly defined problem whose formulation was unfamiliar to them, many good minds failed to grasp its true meaning." (p. 16)

On pages 93-94, Newman stated the issue good minds had difficulty grasp-ing: The issue is not "arguments which issue in the belief of these doctrines, but to investigate what it is to believe in them, what the mind does, what it contemplates, when it makes an act of faith. It is to argue that the same elementary facts which create an object for an assent, also furnish matter for an inference:

and in showing **what we believe,**

I shall unavoidedly be in a measure showing

why we believe;

but this is the reason that makes it necessary for me at the outset to insist on the real distinction between two concurring and coincident courses of thought, . . ." (Italics added)

"Not only in the thing believed,

but also in the ground of belief . . .

only . . . the material object of faith,

with the thing believed,

not with the formed."

"I proceed to show how inferential exercises, as such, always must be conditional."[19]

The key to the relation between assent and inference is the sentence which moves from the same elementary facts to the object for assent and to the matter for inference. Because of this sameness, the reader might confuse the assent and inference as well as the states of mind at issue. Whereas the motives of credibility would be found in the inference, this is not Newman's aim; rather, he is concerned to show us that we can know God's existence so we can assent. Nonetheless he realized that these were concurring and coincident courses of thought. For some reason, Gilson noted the distinction rather than the concurrence. On page 209, there is a section which might have led to the confusion: "I proceed to show how inferential exercises, as such, always must be conditional." These frequent emphases of the conditional are not always qualified as in this case by "as such," nevertheless, they always get us back to the matter for inference rather than to the object for assent.

A challenging question arises from Newman's final page in the **Grammar** where he remarks that there need not be a priority when it comes to reason or faith because "one and the same teaching is in different aspects both object and proof, and elicits one complex act both of inference and of assent."

The contrast between Gilson's explicit statement that there cannot be a complex act both of inference and of assent and Newman's conclusion which states explicitly the opposite indicates there is a possible misunderstanding on Gilson's part. Interestingly, James Collins concludes his treatment of Newman in **God and Philosophy** with the claims that "he seeks to combine the values of all four types of assent," and that "real assent does not wipe out the speculative truth about God and its informal inferential foundation, but it adds the perfection of a practical attachment of our heart to His own personal being."[20]

Collins gives a historical justification for Newman's unification of the four assents. This justification is detailed in the Note Two of the 1880 edition where Newman rejects the claim that he has used only the descending route from atheism.

> 'There is a God,' when really apprehended, is the object of a strong energetic adhesion, which works a revolution in the mind; but when held merely as a notion, it requires but a cold and ineffective acceptance, though it be held ever so unconditionally. . . . It is the normal faith which every Christian has, on which he is stayed, which is his spiritual life, there being nothing in the exposition of the dogmas . . . which does not address the imagination, as well as the intellect.[21]
>
> But the question is whether a real assent to the mystery, as such, is possible; and I say it is not possible, because, though we can imagine the separate

> propositions, we cannot imagine them altogether . . . the spiritual life of the Christian to report upon a real assent, what stands for things, not for notions only, is each of those propositions taken one by one, and that not in the case of intellectual and thoughtful minds only, but of all religious minds whatever, in the case of a child or a peasant, as well as of a philosopher.[22]

> Methodical processes of inference, useful as they are, **as far as they go**, are only instruments of the mind, and need, in order to their due exercise, that real ratiocination and present imagination which gives them a sense beyond their letter, and which, while acting **through** them, reaches to conclusions beyond and above them. Such a living organon is a personal gift, and not a mere method of calculus.[23]

Probably the most important specimen available to clarify Gilson's misunderstanding occurs on page 250. In this specimen, we find Newman affirming the limits of inference, but also the way to the conclusion and the real assent through the processes of inference. By inference alone, ratiocination would not achieve its end. Only by a synthesis of inference and assent do we have the limits passed.

James Collins finds this synthesis the result of the crises Newman faced in his time. "In the synthesis between the informal inference from conscience and the four kinds of assent, Newman finds his fundamental, mature answer to the problem of atheism and philosophical naturalism."[24]

Immediately before this, Collins had summarized the section from page 250 in two sentences. "Yet even our reflective hold on God is not enough when it remains in the speculative mode of a notional assent. The speculative truth about the God-proposition needs to be integrated with a real assent of our mind to God, apprehended as a personal reality."[25]

Collins covers much the same ground in his introduction to **Philosophical Readings in Cardinal Newman** pages 20-24, but it is on this last page that he gives the synthesis:

Newman defends both the distinctive nature of
conscience and its intentional reference to a personal,
good God. After reflecting on the commanding act of
conscience, we can infer the presence of a transcendent
language and judge, can assent in a notional way to
the proposition that God exists, and then give our real
assent to the actuality of God Himself.

Christianity is addressed, both as regards **its
evidences** and **its contents,** to minds which are in the
normal condition of human nature, as believing in God
and in a future judgement. Such minds it addresses
both though the intellect and through the imagination;
creating a certitude of its truth by arguments too various
for direct enumeration, too personal and deep for words,
too powerful and concurrent for refutation. Nor need
reason come first and faith second (though this is the
logical order), but one and the same teaching is in
different aspects both object and proof, and elicits
one complex act both of inference and of assent.[26]

Not as if there were in fact, or could be, any line
of demarcation or party wall between these two modes
of assent, the religious and the logical . . . it does
not interfere with holding that there is a theological
habit of mind, and a religious, each distinct from each,
religion using theology, and theology using religion.[27]

Gilson and Collins unite to clarify the need for care in approaching

Newman's position in the **Grammar** on the distinction and/or separation of

inference and assent and of the various types of assent. Then the method

of thought Newman pursued in answering the issues of liberalism becomes

obvious. But, at the same time, the difficulty one's own antecedent reason-

ings pose for not misunderstanding Newman becomes equally obvious.

Newman's Specimen on Logic

Methods of Thought

Gilbert concluded his **Renaissance Concepts of Method** with a review

of the conflict between educators and methodologists of science. Because

there is a link between the Greeks, Bacon, and the latter's successors,

and because Newman was in opposition to the empiricism of such successors

as Hume and Locke, it will be of value to examine this conclusion and compare it with Newman's treatment of logic on pages 227-228 of the **Grammar.**

The interpreters Gilbert selected divide into two groups: those who studied methodology as an art and those who studied it as a science; the former representing educators who strove to enable themselves and others to carry out their arts into life, the latter who strove to demonstrate and prove through their methods.

Aristotle had placed the former under **Topics** and the latter under **Posterior Analytics.** During the Renaissance, the Humanists frightened the "subject-matter teachers" into making a method which would insure the achievement of knowledge. In this second method we have the beginning of what is now called the scientific method. But in light of the whole controversy we have a continuation of the debate between the pursuers of rhetoric and those of philosophy.

However, the distinction and the separate treatment of methods on the upper and lower levels of education would not care for the inventions either in the arts or in the sciences. Nor the means to determining "the false and invalid from the body of knowledge."[28]

Yet the scientific method presaged in the Renaissance was far from what we have and "when the notion of experimentation begins to be formulated expressly, by Francis Bacon, it is framed not in the terms of the scientific methodology but in those of the artistic methodology."[29] Significant in Bacon was his acceptance of the part Nature was to play in the future of **Topics** as the "respondent" while the scientist took the place of the "challenger." From this arose an emphasis upon knowledge rather than upon its transmission. Therefore the way was open towards an empirical study distinct from dialectic, logic, and discussion, though this was not yet the case.

Because the methods of research and these other methods were readily confused, it is understandable why "the comparison of Aristotle's actual practices with the methods he advocated could be considered, in the Renaissance, a satisfactory empirical test of those methods."[30] Consistency of practice and preaching seemed to constitute the test.

Nonetheless this apparent test was the high mark in the Renaissance move towards an empirical test. At the same time, the methodologists recognized the inadequacy of logic as an inventive process, as well as in the demonstrative. This very excitement over the limits of an arts-methodology did no more than help pass on an "'already established art' and a science methodology in need of invention and demonstration prepared the way for an improved teacher education and an empirical scientific method."[31]

Though the heart of Gilbert's position and results are in the conclusion, one major idea played down there but given prominence in the introduction is the difference between the historian of philosophy and the historian of science. The latter, according to him, "alone is qualified to judge of the contributions made to the techniques and concepts of a science, . . . while the former is responsible for the analysis of ideas about method."[32] The historian of philosophy is responsible for determining the question found in the conclusion: to what extent is there a consistency between what a methodologist claims to be doing and what such a person does. Three possibilities result: there is a consistency; what the historian of science determines after the historian of philosophy concludes are not recognizable; and though the ideas on method are exceptional, the practice is not on a par with it. Gilbert realized that it is a rare person who not only knows the method to be used, but who knows what method is being used.

Newman considered much the same ground on pages 227-228 of the **Grammar**:

Science in all its departments has too much simplicity and exactness, from the nature of the case, to be the measure of fact. In its very perfection lies its incompetency to settle particulars and details.

As to Logic, its chain of conclusions hangs loose at both ends; both the point from which the proof should start, and the points at which it should arrive, are beyond its reach; it comes short both of first principles and of concrete issues.

. . . thought is keen and manifold, its sources are too remote and hidden, its path too personal, delicate, and circuitous, its subject matter too various and intricate, to admit of the trammels of any language, of whatever subtlety and of whatever compass.

Nor is it any disparagement of the proper value of formal reasonings thus to speak of them. That they cannot proceed beyond probabilities is most readily allowed by those who use them most. Philosophers, experimentalists, lawyers, in their several ways, have commonly the reputation of being, at least on moral and religious subjects, hard of belief, because, proceeding in the necessary investigation by the analytical method of verbal inference, they find within its limits no sufficient resources for attaining a conclusion.

Nay, they do not always find it possible in their own special province severally; for, even when in their hearts they have no doubt about a conclusion, still often, from the habit of their minds, they are reluctant to own it, and dwell upon the deficiencies of the evidence, or the possibility of error, because they speak by rule and by book, though they judge and determine by common sense.

Let then our symbols be words: let all thought be arrested and embodied in words. Let language have a monopoly of thought; and thought go for only so much as it can show itself to be worth in language. Let every prompting of the intellect be ignored, every **momentum** of argument be disowned, which is unprovided with an equivalent wording, as its ticket for sharing in the common search after truth. Let the authority of nature, common sense, experience, genius, go for nothing. Ratiocination, thus restricted and put into grooves, is what I have called inference, and the science, which is its regulating principle, is logic.

Newman may have gone too far in limiting science to words, but he recognized the limitation of traditional logic and provided a link between the Renaissance and our modern logic. Thus he is helpful in enabling us to read Victorian authors on education and science. In this section we have had a series of specimens from the **Grammar** which become more intelligible to the ordinary reader by the use of principles, states of mind, and methods of thought. In this section we have had a visual approach to the reading of crucial and difficult specimens of the **Grammar**. The reader should find that the usual block printing of Newman does a disservice to the exquisite care he took to lay out the constructions of his arguments. A combination of the methodology of this work and the several themes which unify it should persuasively provide the reader with an **organon** to read Newman more enjoyably and meaningfully.

An issue which makes principle, states of mind, and methods of thought complexly evident is the conflict between dogma and religion, between theology and religion, between what we know and what we do, between our intellectual, imaginative, and total search for truth. This test case is arranged in a series of dialectical parts. Part one indicates the change from Newman's day to our own in what we assume. Part two examines the issue as complex and accepts this complexity as the key to the **Grammar's** treatment of the issue. Part three alludes to the link between our complex approach to truth and our hope of a solution to our plight. The solution from our vantage point is the complex assent, notional and real, uniting the inference and the assent.

At the end of the section on "Belief in One God," Newman both outlines the moves from Natural Religion and the contemplation this allows and the addition which comes from Christianity to the relation of theology and religion. Step by step he goes through the Old Testament and the New Testament to solve the error of so many who put dogma and a living religion into conflict. He does this by reconciling notional and real assents. Since this teaching is the foundation of a universal spirituality, it is important to take pains with an analysis of what follows upon this outline. On the other hand, Newman's own experiences show through at this point:

> When men begin all their works with the thought
> of God, acting for His sake, and to fulfill His will,
> when they ask His blessings on themselves and their
> lives, pray to Him for the objects they desire, and
> see Him in the event, whether it be according to their
> prayers or not, they will find everything that happens
> tends to confirm them in the truths about Him which
> live in their imaginations, varied and unearthly as
> those truths may be. Then they are brought into His
> presence as that of a Living Person, and are able to
> hold converse with Him, and that with a directness and

simplicity, with a confidence and intimacy, **mutatis mutandis**, which we use with an earthly superior; so that it is doubtful whether we realize the company of our fellowmen with greater keenness than these favoured minds are able to contemplate and adore the Unseen, Incomprehensible Creator.

This experience, then, is presupposed in this test case and is the end to which it is directed.

Part I. Change in Mandala

Gerald Holton noted noted the change from 1850 - 1950 in the world's value system. As he edited the American Academy of Arts and Sciences' seminar **Science and Culture** in 1965, Gerald Holton organized a series of mandala changes from 1850 to that time.

Mandala

From the beginning to the present day, science has been shaped and made meaningful not only by its specific, detailed findings but even more fundamentally by its thematic hypotheses. The reigning themata until about the mid-nineteenth century have been expressed perhaps most characteristically by the mandala of a static, homocentric, hierarchically ordered, harmoniously arranged cosmos, rendered in sharply delineated lines as in those of Copernicus' own handwriting. It was a finite universe in time and space; a divine temple, God-given, God-expressing, God-penetrated, knowable through a difficult process similar to that necessary for entering the state of Grace - by the works of the spirit and the hand. While not complete knowledge, it was as complete as the nature of things admits in this mortal life.

This representation was slowly supplanted by another, increasingly so in the last half of the nineteenth century. The universe became unbounded, 'restless' (to use the fortunate description of Max Born), a weakly coupled ensemble of infinitely many separate, individually sovereign parts and events. While evolving, it is continually interrupted by random discontinuities on the cosmological scale as well as on the submicroscopic scale. The clear lines of the earlier mandala have been replaced by undelineated, fuzzy smears, similar perhaps to the representation of distribution of electron clouds around atomic nuclei.

> And now a significant number of our most thoughtful
> scholars seems to fear that a third mandala is rising
> to take precedence over both of these - the labyrinth
> with the empty center, where the investigator meets
> only his own solutions to his own puzzles. And this
> philosophical threat is thought to be matched, as is
> being suggested by several articles in this issue, by
> the physical threat considered as originating from a
> blind, aimless, self-motivating, ever-growing engine
> of technology.[1]

We are in this relativistic and agnostic period worldwide. Our scientists, our artists, our musicians, our writers, our playwrights, our space efforts, and our entire culture are completing a century and longer move from an authoritarian and absolutistic position to a relativistic position. From a perfectionistic approach to a limited approach.

Newman was already aware of this as he completed the **Grammar,** but this awareness becomes clearer to us through Joyce and Eliot. Between the 1850 mandala and the present mandala we find the second. Here **Ulysses** and **The Wasteland** prepare us. Before World War I we could expect to perfect the world. We could expect to perfect ourselves. After 1922, we could not.

Unfortunately, those who gave us our spirituality for the 20th Century did not realize this. They remained in the first mandala without the insight Newman had. Now with the insight of Joyce, Marilyn French concludes her masterful **The Book as World** with a series of comparisons: "**Ulysses** is a monument to defining morality in a relativistic world. It does not sentimentalize or idealize that world, but neither does it sentimentalize or idealize any past time. While Eliot was seeing fear in a handful of dust, Joyce was seeing eternity in a grain of sand. . . . **Ulysses** is the **Commedia** of the twentieth century, and a far more agreeable one than its predecessor."[2]

Later in the conclusion, French uses the relativistic approach on the reader: "When the narrative style has thrashed this poor wheat into the dust to which we all return, there remains the small, shining, stubborn seeds of human decency, human suffering, human aspirations - the nobility that is the other face of ignominy, the significance contained in a mass of trivia, the godliness shining in a handful of slime. If you can see that godliness, it is your own you are seeing."[3]

Newman gives us the method to see ourselves and all others in this slime. He does this by reviewing the prophets and the Fathers. "If then it be objected that Christianity does not, as the old prophets seem to promise, abolish sin and irreligion within its pale, we may answer, not only that it did not engage to do so, but that actually in a prophetical spirit it warned its followers against the expectation of its so doing."[4] Also, in the same work - we cannot expect perfection. We are what we are or we are nothing. And we certainly are not perfect.

In **The Idea of a University**, Newman showed the limits of education. "Quarry the granite rock with razors, or moor the vessel with a thread of silk; then may you hope with such keen and delicate instruments as human knowledge and human reason to contend against those giants, the passion and the pride of man."[5] The end was the gentleman and this was ambivalent. The gentleman could become a saint or an apostate, a saint or cynic. His image of this is clear.

His spirituality accepts the limits of a universal expectation just as we must accept the limits of a liberal education. These limits require a complex approach as we will see in the next section.

Part II. Complexity is the Key

Newman's spirituality is complex as his thought because it is one with his thought. In the following search for the foundations of his spirituality, we will consider inference and assent, conscience, and the illative sense. These will do well for the educated person. Authority will be necessary

for the uneducated. Thus, a major responsibility, in Newman's approach
is for the educated person to be open to the uneducated. Just as the enlightened must return to the cave, so those who have a developed conscience and
a developed illative sense must return - even at the prospect of death.
Newman, as educator, preacher, and rhetorician, is prepared to share his
spirituality if we will keep the search alive by our expectations. Obviously,
then, any work on his spirituality is but a test case.

Newman does not expect everyone to have a developed illative sense
available for determining their own rule. "The Illative Sense, that is,
the reasoning faculty, as exercised by gifted, or by educated or otherwise
well-prepared minds."[6] "To learn his own duty in his own case, each individual must have recourse to his own rule; and if his rule is not sufficiently
developed in his intellect for his need, then he goes to some other living,
present authority, to supply it for him, not to the dead letter of a treatise
or a code."[7]

How do we prepare our minds for spirituality, according to Newman?
He tells us under "The Sanction of the Illative Sense."

> We are in a world of facts, and we use them; . . . We
> speculate on them at our leisure. . . . we are less
> able to doubt about . . . ourselves. We are conscious
> of the objects of external nature, and we reflect and
> act upon them, and this . . . we call our rationality.
> And we use the . . . elements without first criticiz-
> ing . . . so is it much more unmeaning in us to criticize
> or find fault with our own nature . . . Our being . . . is
> a fact not admitting of question. . . . This is my essen-
> tial stand-point, and must be taken for granted. . . . I
> am what I am, or I am nothing. I cannot think, reflect,
> or judge about my being without starting from the very
> point which I aim at concluding. . . . My first elementary
> lesson of duty is that of resignation to the laws of
> my nature . . . my first disobedience is to be impatient
> at what I am, and to indulge an ambitious aspiration
> after what I cannot be, to cherish a distrust of my
> powers, and to desire to change laws which are identical
> with myself.[8]

From facts to speculation to rationality to acceptance of ourselves. From here we go on to what Newman in **The Idea of a University** calls rare: "self-knowledge, not as a mere end, but as something to be put to use. We can either resign ourselves to this destiny or have a cheerful concurrence in an overruling Providence."[9]

Newman goes on to note that what is natural to us is neither a fault nor an enormity. Nature cannot be at war with itself. Not only are we in accord with nature, but we have a principle of vitality within us by which we are healed and made whole. We can expect that as animals . . . "find their good in the use of their particular nature, is a reason for anticipating that to use duly our own is our interest as well as our necessity."[10]

Newman moves from our nature to our destiny by differentiating us from animals. We are beings who develop. Our development is due to the use we make of our native endowment, of our minds. As Newman has it: "It is his gift to be the creator of his own sufficiency."[11]

At this point, Newman applies the presuppositions to the issue: "this law of progress is carried out by means of the acquisition of knowledge, of which inference and assent are the immediate instruments."[12] Individually and socially, we have a sacred duty to progress and we do this through "the right use of these two main instruments."[13]

As we advance towards our destiny, we are fulfilling a spirituality rooted in the sanction of the Illative Sense. To the degree we understand our pursuit of knowledge, we also understand the basis for Newman's spirituality. The relationship between inference and assent is such that we can save ourselves from false expectations. We must not refuse the obscurity of inference nor the distinctness of assent. Our temptation is to attempt to discover a rule by which to judge by assuming that by the action of

language and inference "the margin disappears . . . between verbal argumentation and conclusions in the concrete."[14] Yet we must "confess that there
is no ultimate test of truth besides the testimony born to truth by mind
itself."[15]

This places a burden upon us since judgment is left to us. When we
preach or counsel, we must realize that we cannot do the work for the other.
The Illative Sense and the development of conscience, as we will soon notice,
are our responsibility, but without preparation, we are inadequate.

For Newman, building up an image is important for a real apprehension
and assent. In regard to historical characters, firsthand experience is
the route, but for God, the route is conscience. After showing the limits
of our response to inanimate objects and even horses and dogs, Newman compares
our image of the divine person to our response to our mothers and fathers.
We can imagine our faults overwhelming us "as on hurting a mother;"[16] and
we can imagine the peace we feel "on our receiving praise from a father."[17]
Our consciences, as dictate, reveal an image of one who is worthy of our
worship; and thus, we have the **principle** of religion.

Whereas the stress upon knowledge seems to ignore the place of the
will in moving towards our destiny, once Newman has cared for the harmony
of the universe and Bacon's rules of understanding, he can display the relationship: "the laws of the mind are the expression, not of mere constituted
order, but of His will."[18] Earlier he had contrasted "bound" and "carried
on." This is most important to grasp for Newman's spirituality. Law does
require its fulfillment, but those under the law need not feel they are
chained. In fact, if they cooperate, the law carries them towards its own
fulfillment.[19] Now he reminds us that one purpose of a law is to inform
us of God. We learn and gain power from a knowledge of the principles.

These principles are unalterable, yes, but we are to use them. As we use them, we possess them. Rather than limiting us, they free us. We freely enjoy them. Nonetheless, our spirituality is not without difficulty. But a proper **state of mind** which Newman is describing in this entire section enables us to welcome the difficulties. The special stress between inference and assent need not lead us to separating them and opposing them; instead to a security that God gave us these instruments and can do with them as He pleases, while we can use them as we find Him.

In accord with Augustine's position, Newman reminds us, too, that "It is He who teaches us all knowledge; and the way by which we acquire it is His way."[20] As we pursue each branch of knowledge in accord with its own principles and methods, we are sure we will receive His blessing, matter for opinion and, at the proper time, for proof and assent. This is why it is necessary for us to study the **Grammar** and how our minds work in every area of knowledge. Whereas this need for His blessing is true in regard to the arts and the sciences, how much more so is there a need for His blessing in religious and ethical inquiries.[21] We welcome the difficulty in pursuing these forms of fulfillment in religious and ethical inquiries. He has made the way a true discipline seemingly on purpose so that as we arrive, we are devoted to Him upon finding Him.[22]

Why is grammar important? To prepare us for the distinctions Newman uses in providing us with an understanding of assent. Why is assent important? To solve the twofold problem: "to determine what a dogma of faith is, and what it is to believe it." Why are inference and assent both important? These are two instruments by which we can pursue the object and the proof.[23] These enable the teaching of Christianity to reach us and this "same teaching is in different aspects both object and proof, and elicits

a complex act both of inference and of assent."[24] Why is this teaching
so important? Because it "speaks to us one by one, and it is received by
us one by one, as the counterpart, so to say, of ourselves, and is real
as we are real."[25] Why does Newman conclude his work with inference and
assent in religion? "In order to show how (he) would apply the principle
of the Essay to the proof of its divine origin."[26] Why do I enter the test
case here? Newman's principles are not only apologetic but pastoral. These
principles can be applied as well to his spirituality.

Newman assumes a believer and one who holds that there is a future
judgment. Then his spirituality can begin, and end, in the person, but
in a person who is supported by others. To come to this, we must see how
Newman considers the search and how he sees his principles.

> And especially, by this disposition of things, shall
> we learn, as regards religious and ethical inquiries,
> how little we can effect, however much we exert ourselves,
> without that Blessing; for, as if on set purpose, He
> has made this path of thought rugged and circuitous
> above other investigations, that the very discipline
> inflicted on our minds in finding Him, may mold them
> into due devotion to Him when He is found. 'Verily
> Thou art a hidden God, the God of Israel, the Saviour,'
> is the very law of which is to lead us to Him; and who
> among us can hope to seize upon the true starting-points
> of thought for that enterprise, and upon all of them,
> who is to understand their right direction, to follow
> them out to their just limits, and duly to estimate,
> adjust, and combine the various reasonings in which
> they issue, so as safely to arrive at what it is worth
> any labour to secure, without a special illumination
> from Himself? Such are the dealings of Wisdom with
> the elect soul. 'She will bring upon him fear, and
> dread, and trial; and She will torture him with the
> tribulation of Her discipline, till She try him by Her
> laws, and trust his soul. Then She will strengthen
> him, and make Her way straight to him, and give him
> joy.'[27]

We begin the search as inquirers. We end the search as assenters.
Between, we carry out innumerable inferences. These were detailed in the
Apologia. We can detail our own.

Part III. Complex Assent

Other than the quotation from John on The Good Shepherd, the **Grammar** ends as follows:

> Nor need reason come first and faith second (though this is the logical order), but one and the same teaching is in different aspects both object and proof, and elicits one complex act both of inference and of assent. It speaks to us one by one, and it is received by us one by one, as the counterpart, so to say, of ourselves, and is real as we are real.[28]

Since Newman had stressed the difference of inference and assent, one conditional and the other unconditional, I returned to "Complex Assent" on pp. 158-159 to clarify my thought. There I found how he keeps the two together. After having achieved assent, one is asked why. Continuing one's assent, the answerer reviews the inference, either as it was originally attained or in an alternative fashion. Upon the completion of the demonstration, one is certain as before and during the process.

Now Newman explains the various distinctions involved in the fact that to assent is not necessarily to prove:

1. One can prove what one assents to because "the conclusiveness of a proposition is not synonymous with its truth."[29]

2. "A proposition may be true, yet not admit of being concluded."[30]

3. It "may be a conclusion and yet not a truth."[31]

Thus Newman recognized the danger of absolutizing the "harmony of the universe" so that the same laws which apply to nature should not be expected to apply to our "modes of thought."

"And more than this, there is that principle of vitality in every being, which is more of a sanative and restorative character . . . to use duly our own is our interest as well as our necessity."[32]

> Natural religion is based upon the sense of sin; it recognizes the disease, but it cannot find, it does but look out for the remedy. That remedy, both for

> guilt and for moral impotence, is found in the central
> doctrine of Revelation, the Mediation of Christ. . . . It
> has with it (Christianity) that gift of staunching and
> healing the one deep wound of human nature. . . .Our
> communion with it is in the unseen, not in the obsolete.
> . . . This power of perpetuating His Image, . . . is
> a grand evidence how well He fulfills to this day that
> Sovereign Mission which . . . has been in prophecy
> assigned to Him.[33]

We begin in need of healing, we experience a principle of vitality within us, we use inference and assent, and we let ourselves be open to illumination; through the Mediation of Christ we are staunched and healed. Then we develop in accord with the Image He offers us: this Image which has held sway in prophecy and in actuality from the beginning. Yet our communion with His presence is unseen. Newman's spirituality is ideal for these, because it accepts our sinfulness, expects us to use inference and assent in accord with the materials we come upon in our search and ends in joy.

TEST CASE ON TIME

"The Second Spring" - Uses of Time:

Real and Apocalyptic

An analysis of the "The Second Spring" revealed the amazing compulsion with time which possessed John Henry Newman. Yet the fact that an analysis of the sermon was necessary in order to reveal these many uses of time makes it obvious that his artistry controlled his compulsions. And a second compulsion became evident from the analysis - that with the apocalyptic. Only through the power of an apocalyptic imagination is the force of the sermon upon its original audience to be explained. His ordinary, Bishop William Ullathorne, reported that the audience, with rare exception, was in tears for half an hour. This artful use of time is beyond the mere phenomenon of time. It is an exceptional instance of the juxtaposition of real and apocalyptic time which is actually an autobiographical awareness of past, present, and future through the symbolical experience of personal and social life. As George Landow explains in **Approaches to Victorian Autobiography:** "To qualify as an autobiography a work must not only present a version, myth, or metaphor of the self, but it must also be retrospective and hence it must self-consciously contrast the two selves."[1] With autobiographical time, we have the basis for a unity of the four classical theories of time Robert Brumbaugh found by his research preliminary to writing his work on Plato's **Parmenides,** which he reported in **Plato On the One.** Time has the appearance of the static field, of the dynamic field, of organic growth, and of the atomic moment. Plato expressed these phenomena in his hypotheses as the now, the volume of duration, age, and the instant.[2] Each by itself is inadequate. Together they are more than phenomena. Here Newman's obsession enabled him to find a sufficiently complex and subtle set of symbols

of time to provide his audience with an experience beyond the phenomena.
Though a study of time in all of his writings would be a worthwhile work,
the seeds of such a study are contained in **The Second Spring**.

1. Unity in "The Second Spring"

On what basis did Newman found the unity of "The Second Spring?" On
the basis of time. Newman contrasts the direction of time in the physical
order with the phenomenon of time in the political order. And he does it
in light of a portent, in light of an apocalyptic understanding, in light
of a combat.

The excellent study of the Apocalypse as **Combat Myth** by Adele Yarbro-
Collins shows the four stages:

Table 1

    a. Threat (vss. 3-4)

    b. Salvation (vss. 5-6)

    c. Combat Victory (vss. 7-9)

    d. Victory of Shout (vss. 10-12)[3]

Chapter 12 of **The Apocalypse** moves between heaven, earth, and the desert.
Time loses its constraining influence. We are in the past, the present,
and future interchangeably. Its boundaries are permeable. We can easily
understand the tears of the original audience if we examine the drama of
"The Second Spring" in this light.

I. Time and the Audience of "The Second Spring"

The audience listens to the touching, memorable verses of the canticle:
Surge, propera, amica mea, columba mea, formosa mea, et veni. They have
contemplated these in their prayer with the experience of a hostile popula-
tion. These verses have given them hope that the Church will eventually
conquer. At the end of the sermon they will realize how Philip Neri has

been with them for some 300 years and how the flowers have been watered by the blood of the English Catholics. But now at the beginning of the sermon, Newman has to sketch, in some detail, the usual order of time.

II. Nature and Time

"We have familiar experience of the order, the constancy, the perpetual renovation of the material order which surrounds us." The contrast between permanency and change appears from a variety of apt symbols including the seasons. And already Newman raises the hope of victory: "We know, withal, that May is one day to have its revenge upon November."

III. Contrasting Time

Next he contrasts the physical order and its cycle with the moral order and its seeming fickleness: now up, then down. But even worse, the political order which is doomed to dissolution. Far worse, human beings, destined to dissolution, decay and death from the moment of conception.

His audience could grant the inevitability of this experience within themselves just as Newman struck them with the memory of their experience of their moral lives: "So is it, too, with our moral being, a far higher and diviner portion of our natural constitution."

Throughout this section Newman carries the drama of life through its stages by a series of contrasts between spring and winter, only to conclude: "For moroseness, and misanthropy, and selfishness, is the ordinary winter of that spring." No wonder, then, that the audience would be moved by his comparison of the growth and decay of our nature and of our political works.

By these comparisons and contrasts, he has prepared his audience: "my Fathers, my Brothers" for "the tension and suspense of personal experience."[4] They have shared the common English experience of the miraculous renovation of the English Church. Thus he contrasts once more the physical, the political with the moral. Finally the statement of the sermon: "The English Church was, and the English Church was not, and the English Church is once again. This is the portent, worthy of a cry. It is the coming in of a Second Spring; it is a restoration in the moral world, such as that which yearly takes place in the physical." For some six sections, Newman had withheld the storyline. The drama entered into the audience's past struggles; now with the victory they were not yet aware of its meaning. Newman gave voice to their victory shout. Its meaning would become clear through the last two thirds of the sermon.

2. Apocalyptic Time

"Three centuries ago, and the Catholic Church . . . stood in this land in pride of place." The entire land brought forth its Saints, its scholars, its bishops seemingly to be endless. But the audience knew this was not to be. "Oh, that miserable day, centuries before we were born!"

Both his audience from within and he, the stranger, from without, could bear witness "to the fact of the utter contempt into which Catholicism had fallen by the time (they) were born." They had become **Roman** Catholics - strangers in their own land. "A **great** change, and **awful** contrast, between the time-honored Church of St. Augustine and St. Thomas, and the poor remnant of their children in the beginning of the nineteenth century."

I. Apocalyptic Voice

To come back to victory from such a defeat was a miracle which required the apocalyptic voice of Bishop Milner to be worthy of such an event. "What would have been the feelings of that venerable man, the champion of God's ark in an evil time, could he have lived to see this day?" His vision and his prophecy of what exactly happened would have stupefied the people of his time - but most especially this very act. "What is that act? It is the first symbol of a new Hierarchy; it is the resurrection of the Church."

II. Apocalyptic Mother

Facing a tearful, awe struck audience, Newman repeated the verses from the Canticle of Canticles, but only after comparing the English Church to an arisen Jerusalem and just before giving the meaning of May having its revenge upon November: "It is the time for thy Visitation. Arise, Mary, and go forth in thy strength into that north country, which once was thine own, and take possession of a land which knows thee not. Arise, Mother of God, and with thy thrilling voice, speak to those who labor with child, and are in pain, till the babe of grace leaps within them. Shine on us . . . till our year is one perpetual May."

The allusions to Apocalypse 12 anticipate Newman's bold treatment in **A Letter to Pusey,** while for his audience they recall his notable treatment of the Blessed Virgin in **An Essay on Christian Development** where, granting the traditional application to the Church, he applies the chapter to Mary so it would have a justification for its application to the Church.

Mary is to fulfill "the promise of this Spring. A second temple rises on the ruins of the old." This demanded the audience let go of the past for a changed future.

Thus Newman prophesied that they would still be liable to martyrdom. Bravely they listened to his concluding questions. "Who is to make you fear? . . . whether to lay the foundations of the Church in tears, or to put the crown upon the work in jubilation?"

III. Apocalyptic Shout

Ordinarily in accord with classical rhetorical practice, the sermon would have ended here and begun with sections 19 and 20, the two concluding sections. In such Newman would have justified himself as a fitting preacher. Instead in the middle of the sermon we found him admitting he was a stranger. At the end he indicates why he is actually not such - he is a token of Philip Neri. This Philip who joined the "**Flores apparuerunt in terra nostra**" of the verse with the salutation, "**Salvete flores martyrum,**" enabled him to join the scriptural declaration of hope with the apocalyptic shout of the Hymn of the Innocents. From a perspective of time, Newman reconciled the three hundred years before, when the temple fell and the same time when Philip began his journey to England from Rome where he had saluted the English missionaries trained at the English college there.

3. Structure of "Second Spring"

We have examined the drama of the sermon by way of time. Not only the spring time of flowers nor the Second Spring, possibly of martyrdom, but in the variety of uses of time paragraph by paragraph. It is time to express explicitly the astounding **structure** of Newman's uses.

I. Apocalyptic Approach to Time

Any process of categorization must be arbitrary, hence we cannot be sure Newman was aware of the following uses, nor can we be sure that these many uses of time were the cause of the profound effect upon his audience which Bishop Ullathorne noted: "'Dr. Newman preached one of his best sermons, and had the bishops and divines - most of them - weeping, for half an hour,'"[5] nonetheless the apocalyptic approach to time is evident in this sermon through its uses.

Uses

Some fifteen uses are obvious from the words themselves: Seasons, History, Time, Age, Years, Months, Day/Night, Life/Death, Young/Old, Centuries, Sun, and Hour. Less obvious from the words themselves is Change. Here verbs and adverbs as well as the context with its contrasts and comparisons make the category evident.

1. Seasons

From the title, we would expect seasons to be crucial. It occurs in some six sections and these the most significant sections of the sermon: section 1, where we are introduced to the theme; section 4, where we are given the outline of the sermon; section 6, where we are prepared for drama and its meaning; section 7, where we are given the periodic statement of the sermon and its title; section 15, where Mary's part in the restoration is highlighted; and section 17, where the challenge of an English springtime is dramatically presented.

2. Time, Years, Day/Night

Three other categories are similarly emphasized: Time, Years, and Days/Nights. These, as a whole, occur in different sections than Seasons. They provide an encompassing pattern of symbols powerful for arousing an historical, yet mythical period for the audience. Time, as in the Apocalypse, is mythical despite the accuracy of the terms for actual events. Time is used in a typical sense rather than a historical - literal.

History occurs more than three times including: as a reward for the limits of the political, as a record against which to compare the unusual experience of the English Church, and as a synonym for a difference in age.

The most frequent category, other than time, because less specific, is Change. Rather than using criteria for development which would have been expected, Newman used change to provide a means to contrast and compare the time from the institution of the English Church, through its fall, and to its resurrection. What is past is past, now for the future. The stranger who is a token of Philip wants the Oratory to "have a name among you, and to be loved by you, and perchance to do you a service, here in your own land." Newman's "The Second Spring" is a perennial service to all who understand English.

These categories can be recalled and appreciated more easily by the use of a table. Table 2 presents both the categories by number of occurrences and the number of the occurrences by each of the 13 categories of uses of time. Several of the more important sections are summed also. Thus we find that sections 15 and 1 have the greatest number of uses. The former is the climax of Bishop Milner's vision of the restoration of the hierarchy. The latter is context of the Second Spring in which the basis of the comparison and the contrast between the orders of the physical, the political, and the moral are set. Sections 4 and 7 are next in number of occurrences. The former is the summary of the sermon. The latter is the rhetorical setting for the drama of the sermon. As for sections 2, 9, and 16, the first completes the contrast of 1, the second describes the change from the English Church at its peak to the depressed state of this Church at their births, and the third is Newman's prophecy of possible persecution. The other sections vary from 9 occurrences to 3. All together there are an astounding 185 uses of time in the sermon.

Table 2
Occurrences of Uses of Time
by Category, Chief Section and Total

Section	1	2	4	7	9	15	16	Total
Time								47
Change								42
Seasons								17
Day/Night								15
Life/Death								14
Young/Old								14
Years								10
Centuries								7
History								5
Hour								4
Months								4
Age								3
Sun								3
	19	12	13	13	12	27	12	185

Time itself occurs on 47 occasions. Nothing is more important in the sermon than time itself. And if the nature as well as the phenomenon of time is considered, much of the 42 occasions of change are really part of the category of time. Rather than considering the criteria of development under change, Newman was concerned with movement for contrast and an atmosphere. The audience was at middle age, they were formed in a church which was dependent upon Vicars Apostolic, now they were to become independent. Yet they could not forget their origins - neither in memory nor in emotions. Thus the third category - seasons - gave Newman an opportunity for his powerful comparison of the life of the church to the changing seasons. Each season had its place in their memories, imaginations, and emotions. Next Day and Night, Life and Death, and Young and Old added the eschatological and apocalyptic elements to their feelings. The repetition of these three categories enabled him to describe the life of the Church and their lives in a moving account of change. Added, once more, to these were the years, the centuries, history, hours, months, ages, and the sun. Fuller and fuller became the experience of time and change.

The metaphor of time, under its many aspects, completed the meaning of the Second Spring. Time with its meaning gave a dramatic unity to this emotional occasion and its interpretation by one who was both a stranger and a brother.

Time has the four appearances Robert Brumbaugh noted: static, dynamic, developmental, and instantaneous. But it also has a variety of forms, e.g., physical, political, moral, and metaphorical. Newman combined these appearances and forms in an amazing unity to dramatize one of the most significant days in English history by recalling the experiences of the earliest days, of the dismal day, of the centuries after this day to Bishop Milner's day,

and finally to the days of his audience. Telescoping these into an overwhelming panorama, he gave meaning to the day in characterizing it as the
start of the Second Spring. And he did this artistically by a surprising
use of time which can now be used to examine this constant in his state
of mind, since obviously only one who was obsessed with the contemplation
of time would have been able to compose a sermon such as this.

Appendix:

Confirmation: Walgrave

Principles, States of Mind, and Methods of Thought

AIM: Newman is one of the great stylists in English literature. As
an intuitive introvert, he brings images from within himself and expresses
his understanding in a narrative style so that the reader will feel the
movement of thought from the unity of his principles.

In Jan Walgrave's "A Psychological Portrait of Newman," we have a study
which confirms the assumptions of this present work. His paper dealt with
Carl Jung's typology. He demonstrated how Newman was both an introvert
and secondary, but that his polarity was such that he brought the dialectical
tension between external reality and his inner life into perfect harmony.

The polarity causes the predominant type to experience a tension with
the lesser type: with Newman, his introversion to feel the opposition of
his matter-of-factness. Whereas Newman preferred to enjoy the fullness
within, he felt obliged to check this with the facts.

"The heart of the whole matter is a state of mind, characterized by
a more or less prolonged hesitation taking place between the moment in which
circumstances urge a person to do something and the moment of his final
decision."[6] This state of mind gave Newman options an extravert would be
likely to omit. During his hesitation, he countered the initial option
with the pro and con of its opposite and from this he came to a catalogue
of aspects of the issue. Probably the most comprehensive set of examples
of this can be found in the **Idea**, where he describes the activities of the
mind successively in relation to truth in itself, to learning, to professions,
and to the many areas which make up a University.

There Newman had the most protracted experience, other than in the Oratory, of a tension between his inner life and the demands of the faculty and others who needed matter of fact guidance. Whether they asked him how to conduct university preaching or relating of their disciplines to others, they knew Newman would be able to balance their introverted and extraverted needs.

Newman was up to such requests because he had a secondary type of character. In a primary character, experiences come and go. Their original impression may well be vivid and powerful, but time erases them as wakefulness cleanses us of the memories of most of our dreams. On the other hand, a secondary type is somewhat more hesitant in reaction, but holds the experience into the future. Such a person cupboards the past for the future. Instead of living in the present on a superficial level, the person lives the past into the present. Proust's **Remembrances of Things Past** names the secondary type.

Walgrave did away with a number of objections to Newman's ways by means of this understanding. Forgetfulness in the extravert contrasts with the phenomenal memory, actually noumenal, of the secondary introvert. Seemingly, Newman held grudges, but in reality he was living as such a type would live. Similarly, Newman's subtlety arose from his ability or talent to step back from an event and flush it out through options and memory.

Combined with these talents was Newman's intuition. Walgrave could have used the example of the **Idea** where Newman held to its history from the days of the Greeks to the Victorian period, instead he used the example from **Development**: "'I have a vivid perception, he says, of the consequences of certain admitted principles, have a considerable capacity of drawing them out.' Yet, on the other hand, still more conspicuous is his gift of penetrating, imaginative intuition grasping in the facts explanatory models and valuational ideas. The way in which he describes the development of Christian doctrine as the expansion of one idea in the mind of the Church is the most convincing illustration of this wonderful capacity."[7]

The intuition could have been a danger rather than a boon if Newman had not combined it with his powerful logic. Logic alone would have lessened what he gained from principles. Intuition alone would have raised his thought too far from the mundane.

Walgrave came upon the basis for Newman's dependence upon Joseph Butler - his polarity of doubt and certitude. Whereas many reading Butler became sceptics and agnostics, Newman deepened his faith and found better ways of expressing the search. Walgrave quotes the famous passage on doubts and difficulties in the **Apologia** after he had worked through Sobry's explanation of Newman's subtlety in the polarity of his striving for unity and his "receptiveness for conflicting impressions."[8]

In other words, as Coleridge and Jung would have it, Newman was gifted by intuition and sensation. The former enabled him to accept options and search for unity, the latter enabled him to accept impressions and express these.[9]

His preference, as an intuitive, for narrative over exposition, was also a preference for a fuller context for his logic, while his polarity came out in his keeping the point fully focused. As he put it, "the tension and suspense of personal observation" are necessary for one's style.

A complement to Walgrave's consideration of Newman's secondariness is Petipas' "Newman's Idea of Literature: a Humanist's Spectrum" which contrasted his criticism with a variety of present day forms of criticism:

> 1. to those extreme realists who debate art by reducing it to but an uninspired reportorial account

of human experience, he insists rather that art instead of merely copying reality was experience for its own distinctive purpose after a pattern of the human mind.

2. to those extreme romantics who enthrone art as a quasi-religion, he assigns it its own distinctive perfection.

3. to those artistic purists who exalt language as an end in itself in literary activity, he recognizes that it must be made subservient to artistic vision.

4. to those depersonalists who mechanize literary activity, he emphasizes that a literary work is essentially a personal expression.

5. to those linguistic technicians who rigidly apply scientific analysis to literary works, he stresses that in genuine artistic expression there will always be a something that ultimately defies analytical explanation.[10]

STYLE: Oscar Wilde wrote an, as he put it, understanding and loving review of Walter Pater's **Appreciations, With an Essay on Style** for the 22 March 1890 **The Speaker**. By a subtle handling of the essay Wilde gave his own position on style. It must be concrete, finely free, the result of an intense vision, beyond mere rhetoric and ornamentation by a love of words and restraint in their use. But the perfect writer will be known, not only by real scholarship, but "by that conscious artistic structure which is the expression of mind in style."[11]

Though the subject at first appeared to Wilde to be too abstract, he found that "in Pater's hands it becomes very real to us indeed . . . behind the perfection of a man's style, must lie the passion of a man's soul."[12] Even Pater's occasional long, convoluted sentences fit his soul: "After a time, these long sentences . . . come to have the charm of an elaborate piece of music, and the unity of such music also."[13]

To conclude the encomium and to give the author upon whose work Pater based his essay, Wilde writes:

> How subtle and certain are his distinctions! If
> imaginative prose be really the special art of this
> century, Mr. Pater must rank amongst our century's most
> characteristic artists. The age has produced wonderful
> prose styles . . . But in Mr. Pater, as in Cardinal
> Newman, we find the union of personality with perfec-
> tion.[14]

Wilde has captured Newman in writing of Pater. Newman's long sentences

repay re-reading and they gain a charm from their music. A rhythmic approach

to prose, as George Saintsbury conducted, reveals the unity of Newman's

prose. The very elaborateness of his style is necessary to provide an instru-

ment for his subtle distinctions. Underneath this unity and subtlety are

both scholarship and a passionate mind; too passionate for a clear explanation

of how it has been achieved.

Wilde had the advantage of living while Newman's writing evidenced

"the union of personality with perfection."[15] We must depend upon those

like Pater and Wilde to witness that unity. We can find the unity in his

style and accept the written signs of that higher unity.

EPILOGUE/ FOREWORD

Study against reading involves a Before, a During, and an After. We move from apprehension to understanding to judgment. Thus this foreword is placed as an epilogue, both before and after. With it we are in a position to review the three parts of this work: the table of contents, the text, and the index. In the table of contents, the headings which are most signifi-cant are highlighted; in the text, a slightly different form of heading is noticed; and in the index, the key terms of both the table of contents and the text are listed together with the names of persons and writings with a review of the entire work under Newman. In this Epilogue/Foreword the chief terms are again highlighted in order to indicate the things to look for in the three parts. The one point left to make is what the advan-tages of specimens and test cases are.

Specimens are examples against which to use **principles, states of mind,** and **methods of thought.** The present set is a starting point for readers to amplify. Because each of us is different, what we collect as specimens will be different; therefore a critical examination of those herein contained will reveal what the reader holds against what the author holds are most important. This will reinforce the significance of the Myers-Brigg approach in the text.

Test cases are partial uses of the approach of the text to the specimens and/or to issues which these specimens broach. Since these are tentative, they are left inconclusive and open. Though some of these may seen irrelevant to some they resulted from questions and references raised by the texts used or by those who have used the texts.

Novum Organon

In order to achieve unity within the complexity of the approach, the relation of whole to part and part to whole must be considered organically. The order of the chapters is due to the **organic style** which unites the various techniques of the work. The **Idea** is the perfect handling of theory, but within this are **specimens** of Newman's use of rhetoric which go beyond the extremely high level of the entire work. In such instances, it is clear that Newman has come upon an **idea** which is worth the greatest pains of rewriting. Usually such instances come where he is concerned that the reader will miss the connection of one part with the others. In other words, his style is **organic**. The specimens which show his highpoints in the **Idea** are the first pages of his introductory chapter and the introduction to Discourse V where he links the first four and the last five discourses in the one principle of the **wholeness** of knowledge. At the end of the section on the **Idea** there is an exceptional specimen from **Historical Sketches** which summarizes the work at its very beginning. Thus Newman's finest examples of rhetoric are his **links** or his **introductions.**

Whereas the **Idea** is crucial for **principle** as the basis of organization, **Callista** is the most sustained use of **states of mind** as an organizing principle. Therefore the long chapter on this work moves repeatedly over the uses of states of mind.

Though in both **Idea** and **Callista rhythm and structure** are significant, this is clearly demonstrated throughout the **Apologia,** however only a small segment of this work is given to show the beauty of this apologetic autobiography because Walter Houghton's **The Art of the Apologia** is available.

While the **Grammar** is a difficult treatise, nonetheless the movement through Newman's rhetorical principles will have prepared the reader to grasp the whole array of helps to gain from this writing despite its difficulty. In fact, even if one does not understand the ideas of the **Grammar** one can learn from the power of its arrangement as well as from its almost endless examples of **methods of thought.**

A rhetorical rarity is the insight from Newman's use of the **Tamworth Reading Room** in the fact that in this chapter there is an example of his using the same material several times and gaining a **different value** from each of its uses. Even more exceptional is the "Second Spring" for demonstrating Newman's willingness to expend all of his rhetorical skill in order to achieve his goals in moving an audience. The tables in this chapter show his **obsession with time** becoming almost a symbol of his subject matter. And in this sermon we have a prime example of **methods of thought** listed in the **Oxford University Sermons.**

Finally, though **Development,** one of Newman's most influential writings, is not the subject matter of the last chapter, nonetheless it is its **theme.** In using this to conclude the work we have come back to one of the major **symbols** of Newman. The rhetoric of this writing developed until it reached its peak in the **Grammar** where Newman gave his one major work which was not called for by controversy or professional need. Thus this last chapter gives us what was most important for his personal life - **spirituality.**

The notes provide the page indications because the **comments** are in the text.

The index indicates the analytic and synthetic aspects of the writing from which the **organic relations** stand out making this a **novum organon.**

The **permissions** are at the end of the work.

NOTES

Introduction

[1]John Morley, **Modern Eloquence** (Philadelphia: J. D. Morris Publishers, 1900), p. 840.

[2]Ibid., p. 91.

[3]Francis Donnelly, **Imitation and Analysis** (Boston: Allyn and Bacon, 1902), pp. 41-42.

[4]Geoffrey Strickland, **Structuralism or Criticism?** (Cambridge, England: Cambridge University Press, 1981), p. 151.

[5]John Henry Newman, **An Essay in Aid of a Grammar of Assent** (Notre Dame, IN: University of Notre Dame Press, 1979), p. 379.

[6]Noel Annan, **Selected Writings in British Intellectual History** (Chicago: University of Chicago Press, 1979), p. 159.

[7]Martin Amis, "Broken Lance," **The Atlantic**, March 1986, p. 106.

[8]Walter Pater, **Appreciations: With an Essay on Style** (New York: Macmillan, 1901), p. 14.

[9]Herbert Read, **English Prose Style** (New York: Pantheon Books, 1952), p. 183.

[10]John Henry Newman, **Apologia Pro Vita Sua: Being a History of His Religious Opinions** (New York: Longmans, Green and Co., 1947), p. 371.

[11]Ibid., p. 366.

[12]Ibid., p. 84.

[13]Ibid., p. 119.

[14]Ibid., p. 84.

[15]Gordon Harper, **Cardinal Newman and William Froude: A Correspondence** (Baltimore: John Hopkins Press, 1933), pp. 22-23.

[16]**Apologia,** p. 372.

[17]Ibid., p. 341.

[18]Ibid., p. 340.

[19]John Henry Newman, **The Idea of a University** (Garden City, NY: Doubleday Press, 1959), p. 4.

[20]Ibid., pp. 74-75.

[21]Ibid., p. 83.

[22]Ibid., p. 85.

[23]Ibid., p. 89.

[24]Ibid., pp. 134-135.

[25]Ibid.

[26]**Essays Critical and Historical** (London: Longmans, Green and Co.), p. 229.

[27]Ibid.

[28]Maisie Ward, **Young Mr. Newman** (London: Sheed and Ward, 1948), p. 294.

[29]Ibid.

[30]Ibid.

[31]**Grammar**, p. 27.

[32]Ibid.

[33]Bertrand Russell, **The Autobiography of Bertrand Russell** (Boston: Little and Brown Publishers, 1967), p. 190.

[34]Ibid.

[35]**Grammar**, p. 176.

[36]Northrop Frye, **T. S. Eliot** (New York: Capricorn Books, 1972), p. 85.

[37]Plato, **Meno**, 89c.

[38]William Buckler, **Prose of the Victorian Period** (Cambridge, MA, 1958), pp. 18-19.

[39]Charles Harrold, **English Prose of Victorian Era** (New York: Oxford University Press, 1951), p. lxxx.

[40]Pater, **Appreciations: With an Essay on Style**, p. 14.

[41]Samuel Wilberforce, "On Cardinal Newman," **Famous Reviews**, edited by R. Brimley Johnson, 1914 (Freeport, NY: Books for Libraries Press, Inc., 1967), p. 289.

[42]Ibid.

[43]Read, p. 183.

[44]Ibid., p. 180.

[45]John Henry Newman, **Autobiographical Writings** (New York: Sheed and Ward, 1957).

[46]Read, pp. 180-181.

[47]Ibid.

[48]Leonard Woolf, "English Prose Style," **The Nation and Athenaeum,** June 23, 1928, p. 2.

[49]Ibid.

Idea

[1]John Henry Newman, **The Idea of a University** (Garden City, NY: Double-day Press, 1959), pp. 10-11.

[2]Gilbert Garraghan, **Literature of Cardinal Newman** (New York: Schwartz, Kerwin, and Fauss, 1912), p. 44.

[3]Derek Sanford and Muriel Spark, **Selected Letters** (New York: Knopf Publishers, 1968), p. 159.

[4]John Henry Newman, **Apologia pro Vita Sua: Being a History of his Religious Opinions**, edited by Charles Harrold (New York: Longmans, Green and Co., 1947), p. 1.

[5]Herbert Read, **English Prose Style** (New York: Pantheon Books, 1952), pp. 182-183.

[6]Garraghan, p. 44.

[7]James Stuart Mill, **Autobiography** (London: Longmans, Green, Reader, and Dyer, 1874), pp. 152-153.

[8]**Idea**, p. 109.

[9]John Henry Newman, **Oxford University Sermons** (New York: Longmans, Green, and Co., 1923), p. 281.

[10]Ibid.

[11]Ibid., p. 263.

[12]Mary Durkin, **Introductory Studies in Newman: With Introduction, Notes, and Inductive Questions** (New York: Scribner Publishing, 1934), p. ix.

[13]Ibid., pp. x-xi.

[14]**Idea**, p. 104.

[15]Ibid., pp. 104-105.

[16]Gertrude Himmelfarb, 'From Clapham to Bloomsbury,' **Commentary**, February 1985, pp. 38, 39.

[17]Noel Annan, **Selected Writings in British Intellectual History** (Chicago: University of Chicago Press, 1979), p. 44.

[18]Himmelfarb, pp. 38, 39.

[19]Ibid., p. 40.

[20]Ibid., p. 45.

[21]Ibid.

Apologia

[1]John Henry Newman, **Apologia Pro Vita Sua, Being a History of his Religious Opinions** (New York: Longmans, Green and Co., 1947), p. 102.

[2]Ibid., p. 106.

[3]Ibid., p. 108.

[4]Ibid., p. 106.

[5]Arthur Galton, **English Prose** (London: B. W. Scott, 1888), p. xiv.

[6]Walter Houghton, **The Victorian Frame of Mind** (New Haven: Yale University Press, 1957), p. 22.

[7]Ibid., p. 424.

[8]Walter Houghton, **The Art of Newman's Apologia** (New Haven: Yale University Press, 1945), p. vii.

[9]Ibid., p. viii.

[10]Ibid., p. 79.

[11]Charles Harrold's review copy of Walter Houghton's **The Art of Newman's Apologia, Modern Language Notes**, 1945, p. 13.

[12]Houghton, **The Art of Newman's Apologia**, p. 34.

[13]Ibid., pp. 100, 30-34.

[14]Ibid., p. 22.

[15]Ibid., pp. 22-23.

[16]Ibid., p. 49.

[17]Ibid.

[18]Harrold, review of **The Art of Newman's Apologia**, p. 214.

[19]Houghton, **The Art of Newman's Apologia**, p. 46.

[20]Harrold, review of **The Art of Newman's Apologia**, p. 214.

[21]Houghton, **The Art of Newman's Apologia**, p. 47.

[22]Ibid., p. 47 ff.

[23]Ibid., p. 48.

[24]Harrold, review of **The Art of Newman's Apologia**, p. 215.

[25]Ibid., p. 214.

[26]Houghton, **The Art of Newman's Apologia**, p. 49.

[27]Ibid., p. 48.

[28]Ibid., p. 49.

[29]Ibid., p. 53.

[30]Ibid.

[31]Ibid., pp. 53-54.

[32]Ibid., pp. 55-56.

[33]Ibid., p. 56.

[34]Ibid.

[35]Harrold, review of **The Art of Newman's Apologia**, p. 214.

[36]Houghton, **The Art of Newman's Apologia**, pp. 7-9.

[37]Ibid., p. 10.

[38]Ibid., p. 19.

[39]Ibid., p. 20.

[40]Ibid., p. 112.

[41]Ibid., pp. 47-48.

[42]Ibid., p. 49.

[43]Ibid., p. 62.

[44]Ibid., p. 67.

[45]Ibid., p. 66.

[46]Ibid., p. 28.

[47]Ibid., p. 30.

[48]Ibid., p. 33.

[49]Ibid., p. 34.

[50]Harrold, review of **The Art of Newman's Apologia**, p. 214.

Callista

[1]Italo Calvino, "Manzoni's **The Betrothed** The Novel of Ratios of Power," in **Use of Literature**, trans. Patrick Creagh (New York: Harcourt Brace Jovanovich, 1986), pp. 197-198.

[2]Alessandro Manzoni, **The Betrothed** trans. Archibald Colquhoun (New York: E. P. Dutton and Co., 1951), pp. 413-414.

[3]Fairbarn quoted in John Henry Newman **An Essay in Aid of a Grammar of Assent** (Notre Dame: University of Notre Dame Press, 1979), p. 382.

[4]Ibid., p. 385.

[5]Ibid., p. 389.

[6]Ibid., p. 198.

[7]Ibid., p. 199.

[8]Ibid., p. 200.

[9]Ibid.

[10]Ibid., p. 202.

[11]Ibid., p. 205.

[12]Ibid., p. 216.

[13]Ibid., p. 217.

[14]Ibid., p. 227.

[15]Ibid., p. 232.

[16]Ibid., p. 233.

[17]Ibid., p. 240.

[18]Ibid.

[19]John Henry Newman, **Callista: A Tale of the Third Century** (New York: Longmans, Green and Co., 1901), p. 110.

[20]**Grammar of Assent**, pp. 97-98.

[21]John Henry Newman, **An Essay on the Development of Christian Doctrine** (Westminster, MD: Christian Classics, 1968) Introduction.

[22]Ibid., p. 10.

[23]Geoffrey Faber, **Oxford Apostles** (New York: Scribner Publishing, 1934), p. xiii.

[24]John Henry Newman, **Oxford University Sermons** (New York: Longmans, Green and Co., 1958), pp. 230, 233.

[25]Ibid., p. 234.

[26]Ibid., p. 237.

[27]George Klubertanz **Philosophy of Human Nature** (New York: Appleton Century, 1953), pp. 389-390.

[28]**Callista**, pp. 78-79.

[29]Ibid., p. 88.

[30]Ibid.

[31]Ibid., p. 95.

[32]Ibid., p. 118.

[33]Ibid., pp. 126-127.

[34]Ibid., p. 127.

[35]Ibid., p. 131.

[36]Ibid., p. 133.

[37]Ibid.

[38]Ibid., p. 127.

[39]Ibid., p. 133.

[40]Ibid., p. 140.

[41]Ibid., p. 190.

[42]Ibid., p. 192.

[43]Ibid., p. 194.

[44]Ibid., p. 218.

[45]Ibid., p. 219.

[46]Ibid., p. 291.

[47]Ibid., p. 252.

[48]Ibid., p. 325.

[49]Ibid., p. 328.

[50]Ibid., p. 354.

[51]Ibid., p. 335.

[52]Ibid., p. 367.

Grammar

[1]Seymour Sarason, **Psychological Problems in Mental Deficiency** (New York: Harper and Row Publishers, 1968), p. 290.

[2]James Collins, "The Heart's Way to God: Newman and the Assent to God," **God and Modern Philosophy** (Chicago: H. Regnery Co., 1959), p. 368.

[3]John Henry Newman, **Oxford University Sermons** (New York: Longmans, Green and Co., 1958), p. 253.

[4]John Henry Newman, **An Essay in Aid of a Grammar of Assent** (Notre Dame, IN: University of Notre Dame Press, 1979), p. 379.

[5]John Henry Newman, **An Essay on the Development of Christian Doctrine** (Westminster, MD: Christian Classics, 1968), p. 181.

[6]Ibid., p. 182.

[7]John Henry Newman, **Apologia Pro Vita Sua, Being a History of his Religious Opinions** (New York: Longmans, Green and Co., 1947), p. 23.

[8]**Development of Christian Doctrine**, p. 325.

[9]James Strachey, **Collected Papers**, Volume 1 (London: Hogarth Press, 1925-1950), p. 3.

[10]James Collins, **Philosophical Readings in Cardinal Newman** (Chicago: H. Regnery Co., 1961), pp. 27-28.

[11]**Grammar of Assent**, p. 379.

[12]Karl Rahner, **Pastoral Approach to Atheism** (New York: Pantheon Books, 1952), p. 1.

[13]Gordon Harper, **Cardinal Newman and William Froude: A Correspondence** (Baltimore: John Hopkins Press, 1933), p. 135.

[14]Ibid., p. 180.

[15]Etienne Gilson, **Introduction of a Grammar of Assent** (Image, 1955), p. 9.

[16]Ibid., p. 11.

[17]Ibid., p. 27.

[18]**Oxford University Sermons**, p. xvi.

[19]**Grammar of Assent**, p. 209.

[20]Collins, **God and Philosophy**, pp. 368-369.

[21]**Grammar of Assent**, p. 112-133.

[22]Ibid., p. 116.

[23]Ibid., p. 250.

[24]Collins, **God and Philosophy**, p. 369.

[25]Ibid.

[26]Collins, **Philosophical Readings in Cardinal Newman**, p. 379.

[27]Ibid., p. 93.

[28]Neal Gilbert, **Renaissance Concepts of Method** (New York: Columbia University Press, 1960), p. 223.

[29]Ibid.

[30]Ibid.

[31]Ibid.

[32]Ibid., p. xix.

Spirituality

[1]Gerald Holton, "Introduction to the Issue 'Science and Culture'," **Daedalus** (Winter, 1965), pp. XXV-XXVI.

[2]Marilyn French, **The Book as World** (Cambridge, MA: Harvard University Press, 1976), p. 37.

[3]Ibid., p. 268.

[4]John Henry Newman, **An Essay in Aid of a Grammar of Assent** (Notre Dame, IN: University of Notre Dame Press, 1979), p. 353.

[5]John Henry Newman, **Idea of a University** (Garden City, NY: Christian Classics Inc., 1968), p. 91.

[6]**Grammar of Assent**, p. 283.

[7]Ibid., p. 279.

[8]Ibid., p. 273.

[9]Ibid., p. 275.

[10]Ibid., p. 273.

[11]Ibid., p. 274.

[12]Ibid.

[13]Ibid., p. 282.

[14]Ibid., p. 275.

[15]Ibid., p. 101.

[16]Ibid., p. 274.

[17]Ibid.

[18]Ibid., p. 276.

[19]Ibid.

[20]Ibid.

[21]Ibid., p. 274.

[22]Ibid., p. 379.

[23]Ibid.

[24]Ibid.

[25]Ibid., p. 301.

[26]Ibid., p. 379.

[27]Ibid., p. 275.

[28]Ibid., p. 379.

[29]Ibid., p. 158.

[30]Ibid., p. 159.

[31]Ibid.

[32]Ibid., p. 273.

[33]Ibid., p. 375.

Test Case on Time

[1]George Landow, **Approaches to Victorian Autobiography** (Athens, OH: Ohio University Press, 1979), p. xiii.

[2]Robert Brumbaugh, **Plato On the One: the Hypotheses in the Parmenides** (New Haven: Yale University Press, 1961), p. 225.

[3]Adele Yarbo-Collins, **Combat Myth in the Book of Revelations** (Missoula, MT: Scholars Press, 1976), p. 232.

[4]John Henry Newman, **The Idea of a University** (Garden City, NY: Doubleday Press, 1959), p. 162.

[5]John Henry Newman, **The Second Spring** (New York: Longmans, Green and Co., 1923), p. 41.

[6]Jan Walgrave, **John Henry Newman: Theologian and Cardinal** (Roma: Urbaniana University Press, 1981), p. 160.

[7]John Henry Newman, **An Essay on the Development of Christian Doctrine** (Westminster, MD: Christian Classics, 1968), p. 167.

[8]Walgrave, p. 160.

[9]Carl Jung, "Psychological Types," **English Prose Style** (New York: Panteon Books, 1952), p. 85.

[10]Joseph Houtart, **John Henry Newman** (St. Louis: Herder, n.d.), p. 69.

[11]Oscar Wilde, **The Speaker,** March 22, 1890, p. 319.

[12]Ibid.

[13]Ibid., pp. 319-320.

[14]Ibid., p. 320.

[15]Ibid.

BIBLIOGRAPHY

Annan, Noel. **Selected Writings in British Intellectual History.** Chicago: University of Chicago Press, 1979.

Brumbaugh, Robert. **Plato On the One: the Hypotheses in the Parmenides.** New Haven: Yale University Press, 1961.

Buckler, William. **Prose of the Victorian Period.** Cambridge, Massachusetts, 1958.

Buckler, William. **The Victorian Imagination.** New York: New York University Press, 1980.

Butler, Joseph. **The Analogy of Religion.** New York: F. Ungar Publishing Co., 1961.

Calvino, Italo. "Manzoni's 'The Betrothed': The Novel of Ratios of Power," **Use of Literature.** Trans. Patrick Creagh. New York: Harcourt Brace Jovanovich, 1986.

Carlyle, Thomas. **Sartor Resartus.** Philadelphia: H. Altemus, 1900.

de Chardin, Teilhard. **The Phenomenon of Man.** New York: Harper Publishers, 1959.

Collins, Adele Yarbo-. **Combat Myth in the Book of Revelation.** Missoula, Montana: Scholars Press, 1976.

Collins, James. **God and Modern Philosophy.** Chicago: H. Regnery Co., 1959.

Collins, James. **Philosophical Readings in Cardinal Newman.** Chicago: H. Regnery Co., 1961.

Craik, George, edited by Henry Craik. **A Manual of English Literature and of the History of the English Language.** 9th edition. London: Griffin and Co., 1883.

Donnelly, Francis. **Imitation and Analysis.** Boston: Allyn and Bacon, 1902.

Durkin, Mary. **Introductory Studies in Newman: with Introduction, Notes, and Inductive Questions.** New York: Benziger Brothers, 1929.

Faber, Geoffrey. **Oxford Apostles: a Character Study of the Oxford Movement.** New York: Scribner Publishing, 1934.

French, Marilyn. **The Book as World: James Joyce's Ulysses.** Cambridge: Harvard University Press, 1976.

Frye, Northrop. **T. S. Eliot.** New York: Capricorn Books, 1972.

Galton, Arthur. **English Prose.** London: B. W. Scott, 1888.

Garraghan, Gilbert. **Literature of Cardinal Newman**. New York: Schwartz, Kerwin, and Fauss, 1912.

Gilbert, Neal. **Renaissance Concepts of Method**. New York: Columbia University Press, 1960.

Harrold, Charles. **English Prose of Victorian Era**. New York: Oxford University Press, 1951.

Harrold, Charles. **A Newman Treasury**. New Rochelle, N.Y.: Arlington House, 1943.

Holton, Gerald. **Science and Culture**. Boston: Beacon Press, 1965.

Hopkins, Gerard Manley and C. C. Abbott. **Further Letters of Gerard Manley Hopkins**. London: Oxford University Press, 1938.

Houghton, Walter. **The Art of Newman's Apologia**. New Haven: Yale University Press, 1945.

Houghton, Walter. **The Victorian Frame of Mind**. New Haven: Yale University Press, 1957.

Hutton, Richard. **John Henry Newman**. New York: Warner Classics, 1899.

Joyce, James. **The Portrait of the Artist as a Young Man**. New York: Viking Press, 1964.

Joyce, James. **Ulysses**. New York: Modern Library, 1946.

Landow, George P. **Approaches to Victorian Autobiography**. Athens, Ohio: Ohio University Press, 1979.

Lawrence, Karen. **The Odyssey of Style in Ulysses**. Princeton, N.J.: Princeton University Press, 1981.

Lonergan, Bernard. **Insight: A Study of Human Understanding**. New York: Philosophical Library, 1957.

Manzoni, Alessandro. **The Betrothed**. New York: Catholic Publication Society, 1900.

Mill, John Stuart. **Autobiography**. London: Longmans, Green, Reader, and Dyer, 1874.

Newman, John Henry. **Apologia Pro Vita Sua, Being a History of his Religious Opinions**. New York: Longmans, Green and Co., 1947.

Newman, John Henry. **The Arians of the Fourth Century**. New York: Longmans, Green and Co., 1919.

Newman, John Henry. **Autobiographical Writings**. New York: Sheed and Ward, 1957.

Newman, John Henry. **Callista: A Tale of the Third Century.** New York: Longmans, Green and Co., 1901.

Newman, John Henry. **Discourses to a Mixed Congregation.** New York: Longmans, Green and Co., 1906.

Newman, John Henry. **The Dream of Gerontius.** Philadelphia: Lippincott, 1911.

Newman, John Henry. **An Essay in Aid of a Grammar of Assent.** Notre Dame, Ind.: University of Notre Dame Press, 1979.

Newman, John Henry. **An Essay on the Development of Christian Doctrine.** Westminster, Md.: Christian Classics, 1968.

Newman, John Henry. **Favorite Newman Sermons.** New York: Spiritual Book Associates, 1940.

Newman, John Henry. **The Idea of a University.** Garden City, N.Y.: Doubleday Press, 1959.

Newman, John Henry. **Introductory Studies in Newman**. New York: Benziger Brothers, 1929.

Newman, John Henry. **Lead, Kindly Light.** Westminster, Md.: Newman Press, 1958.

Newman, John Henry. **A Letter to Pusey.** New York: Longmans, Green and Co., 1888.

Newman, John Henry. **Letters and Diaries of John Henry Newman.** New York: T. Nelson, 1961.

Newman, John Henry. **Literature: A Lecture by Cardinal Newman.** New York: Schwartz, Kirwin and Fauss, 1912.

Newman, John Henry. **Loss and Gain.** New York: Longmans, Green and Co., 1893.

Newman, John Henry. **Oxford University Sermons.** New York: Longmans, Green and Co., 1958.

Newman, John Henry. **The Second Spring.** New York: Longmans, Green and Co., 1923.

Newman, John Henry. **The Via Media of the Anglican Church.** New York: Longmans, Green and Co., 1891.

O'Connell, Marvin Richard. **The Oxford Conspirators.** New York: MacMillan, 1969.

Ong, Walter. **Orality and Literacy.** New York: Melhuen, 1982.

Pater, Walter. **Marius the Epicurean.** New York: Modern Library, n.d.

Pater, Walter. **Appreciations: With an Essay on Style.** New York: MacMillan, 1901.

Plato. **Meno.**

Plato. **Parmenides.**

Plato. **The Republic.**

Plato. **Statesman.**

Proust, Marcel and Joseph Wood Krutch. **Remembrance of Things Past.** New York: Random House, 1934.

Rahner, Karl. **Pastoral Approach to Atheism.** New York: Paulist Press, 1967.

Read, Herbert. **English Prose Style.** New York: Pantheon Books, 1952.

Reed, Thomas et al. **Modern Eloquence.** Philadelphia: J.D. Morris Publishers, 1900.

Russell, Bertrand. **The Autobiography of Bertrand Russell.** Boston: Little and Brown Publishers, 1967.

Sanford, Derek and Muriel Spark. **Selected Letters.** New York: Knopf Publishers, 1968.

Sarason, Seymour. **Psychological Problems in Mental Deficiency.** New York: Harper and Row Publishers, 1968.

Sheehan, Vincent. **Lead, Kindly Light.** New York: Random House, 1949.

Stephen, Leslie. **An Agnostic's Apology.** London: Smith, Elder, 1893.

Sternfeld, Robert and Harold Zyskind. **Plato's Meno.** Carbondale, Il.: Southern Illinois University Press, 1978.

Strickland, Geoffrey. **Structuralism or Criticism?** Cambridge, England: Cambridge University Press, 1981.

Ward, Maisie. **Young Mr. Newman.** London: Sheed and Ward, 1948.

Wilberforce, Samuel. "On Cardinal Newman," **Famous Reviews.** Edited by R. Brimley Johnson, 1914. Freeport, N.Y.: Books for Libraries Press, Inc., 1967.

PERMISSIONS

Vitae Scholasticae, granted permission to publish "An Academic Coverup in Autobiography and Its Reviewing: Newman's Challenge" which appeared in Volume 2 Number 1 Spring 1983 as cited in the footnote at the end of the pertinent chapter.

The two page excerpt on pages 42-44 is from **English Prose Style** by Herbert Read. Copyright (c) 1952 by Herbert Read and renewed (c) 1980 by Benedict Read. Reprinted by permission of Pantheon Books, a Division of Randon House, Inc.

The two page excerpt from "Science and Culture" from Winter 1965 **Daedalus** by permission of American Academy of Arts and Sciences from the Introduction by Gerald Holton.

CHICANO SPEECH
IN THE BILINGUAL CLASSROOM

Edited by Denis J. Bixler-Márquez and Jacob Ornstein-Galicia
with a preface by Robert L. Politzer

American University Studies: Series VI (Foreign Language Instruction).
Vol. 6
ISBN 0-8204-0475-6   200 pages   hardback US $ 38.50*

*Recommended price – alterations reserved

This collection of articles conveys information to teachers and teacher trainers about Chicano Spanish and English in bilingual education and ESL. The first section enables the reader to acquire an understanding of the social and educational issues involved in establishing a role for any given variety of Chicano speech. The second section provides research about Chicano Spanish and English, their distribution, characteristics, and pertinent potential for educational applications. The reader can then proceed to section three and analyze instructional issues, suggested applications, and options for Chicano speech in the bilingual classroom. A select bibliography completes this volume.

PETER LANG PUBLISHING, INC.
62 West 45th Street
USA – New York, NY 10036

Mary E. Bredemeier

URBAN CLASSROOM PORTRAITS
Teachers Who Make a Difference

American University Studies: Series XIV (Education). Vol. 11
ISBN 0-8204-0651-1   279 pages   hardback US $ 38.50*

*Recommended price – alterations reserved

Urban Classroom Portraits begins with a summary of the research on effective schools and classrooms and outlines a theory for urban education. Seventeen profiles of successful urban teachers follow; based on observations and interviews, these often let the teachers speak for themselves. The last chapter considers the range of skills and personal qualities which enable some teachers to be successful against the odds.

Contents: Guiding theory; factors making for effective urban teaching; seventeen teacher profiles; commonalities and differences. Uniqueness of book: Integrates research, theory, and practice; outlines guiding theory; reports teachers' philosophies and practices; summarizes reasons for success.

PETER LANG PUBLISHING, INC.
62 West 45th Street
USA – New York, NY 10036

Bette P. Goldstone

LESSONS TO BE LEARNED
A Study of Eighteenth Century English Didactic Children's Literature

American University Studies: Series XIV (Education). Vol. 7
ISBN 0-8204-0140-4   240 pages   hardback US $ 26.50*

*Recommended price – alterations reserved

Lessons to be Learned is a study of late eighteenth century English didactic children's literature. Through an investigation of social-historical trends, contemporary conceptualizations of childhood, reprinting data and critical reviews, the author shows that these books are far more important than previously believed. Stories by Mrs. Trimmer, Maria Edgeworth, Mrs. Barbauld, Mary Jane Kilner and Dorothy Kilner were not only read and enjoyed by many generations of children, but also helped define the genre of children's literature. *Lessons to be Learned* is invaluable for correcting misconceptions about this seminal literary period, and for raising important questions about how scholars should define and study children's literature.

PETER LANG PUBLISHING, INC.
62 West 45th Street
USA – New York, NY 10036